This book will make _you_ Rich!

Roderich Masters

THE
RODERICK MASTERS
BOOK OF
MONEY-MAKING
SCHEMES

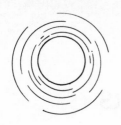

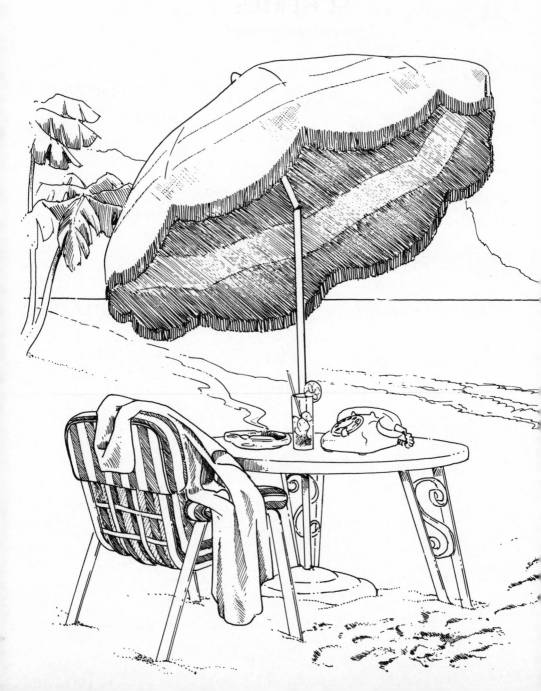

THE
RODERICK MASTERS
BOOK OF
MONEY-MAKING
SCHEMES

OR
HOW TO BECOME
ENORMOUSLY WEALTHY
WITH VIRTUALLY
NO EFFORT

ROUTLEDGE & KEGAN PAUL
LONDON AND HENLEY

● First published in 1981
by Routledge & Kegan Paul Ltd,
39 Store Street, London WC1E 7DD and
Broadway House, Newtown Road,
Henley-on-Thames, Oxon RG9 1EN

● Set in Palatino by
Input Typesetting Ltd, London SW19 8DR

● Printed in Great Britain by
Robert Hartnoll Ltd, Bodmin, Cornwall

● British Library Cataloguing in Publication Data

Masters, Roderick
The Roderick Masters book of money-making schemes
1. Success
I. Title
650.1   HF5386

ISBN 0-7100-0973-9

To Jarvis

CONTENTS

CONTENTS

'ONLY ONE THING IS TWICE AS PLEASURABLE AS DEALING, AND
THAT IS DOUBLE DEALING' R.M.

First Principles:

HOW
TO BECOME
HUGELY
AFFLUENT

Only Money makes you rich. This book is the distillation of a lifetime's experience in the pursuit of the **High Denomination Note**. I will explain from first principles, and from exclusive, practical examples, how YOU can join the exclusive *coterie* that never seems to do much except cruise around in custom-made Mazeratis in the Mediterranean.

Many people seem to suffer from the delusion that it is very difficult to become extremely wealthy. This is wrong. It is an idea put about by the Rich to make the Poor feel bad about being poor, an additional burden to be carried on top of their habitual lack of cash. If the Poor realised how easy it is to grow rich they would very quickly become so; and the Rich would then have to become even richer so that they could go on feeling good about being better off than their fellows. This is known as the *poverty trap*.

In fact, it is remarkably easy to become extraordinarily well-heeled.

I have proved this many times in the course of a career that has spanned the five continents, often two or three at the same time. Making money is not a question of effort: it is a matter of common observation that the main effort in the lives of the Rich is trying to decide between luncheon at the Clochard Enchainé or the Grenouille de Descartes. The equation Hard Work = Money is one of the great illusions of History (*The First Financial Fallacy*). It is perfectly obvious that the Guatemalan waiters at the Clochard Enchainé work hard, 12-hour shifts, with only the odd half-hour off to nip to Fortnum's to top up the smoked salmon supply, yet never in their lives do they get to sit down to enjoy the food. Even if they did, they would probably be too dead-beat to enjoy it. The truth is that hard work, except for the briefest period of entrepreneurial excitement, is a positive *disadvantage* for waxing wealthy. Many of my finest deals have been conducted in a state that to an untrained eye would resemble coma.

> 'THE POOR ARE ALWAYS WITH US; THE RICH ARE ALWAYS
> SOMEWHERE ELSE' R.M.

There is also a misconception that the Rich form an exclusive club, to which no stranger is admitted. This is *The Second Financial Fallacy*. I have proved on many occasions that a crate of Dom Perignon or a Fabergé *objet* dropped in the right quarter opens doors or oils wheels that are normally closed or stuck respectively. This book will be *your* passport to those circles which lead secret and arcane lives in the Corridors of Power, and which you can read about on the social pages of your evening paper. Money is the great lubricant: make sure *you* do not finish up as the greasy stain on somebody else's rag.

All the beginner needs is a genuine love for the rustling sound made by crisp, new notes. Those who are unmoved by the sight of a plump wallet should read no further.

The *Third Financial Fallacy* is that only money begets money: you have to be rich to get richer. This is hugely misguided. In my own lifetime I have made and lost fortunes at such a rate that I frequently find it difficult to remember whether I am extraordinarily flush or penniless at any one time. Either way it does not matter because my credit is impeccable. The fallacy is revealed in its true colours by the application of a little *logic*, which together with *flair*, is the entrepreneur's greatest asset. If money alone bred more money then the same few families would have had the lions' share of the *Grand Crus Classés* and Beluga caviare ever since Man first distinguished him-

2

selffrom the humble beasts by eating them. Yet study of primitive tribes shows that our forebears probably had very little in the way of realisable assets other than flint axe heads, and hollow tubes for tootling upon. Rothschilds and Joe Soap were all one under the loincloth, although I suppose that the former might have started a Flint Bank even then. So it follows that numerous enterprising individuals since those primeval days have done what all mankind is free to do: made a pile. The names of most of these aspiring primitives have been lost in the mists of time, but a few linger on in the names of the vast enterprises they initiated: AMOCO, GEC, QANTAS and so on.

My friend Jarvis (now Lord M*****) rose from a background so obscure that even *he* cannot remember which of several parking lots he was born on, nor whether his mother was the arsonist, his father the poisoner, or vice versa. He seemed doomed to a life of dingy back rooms and short prison sentences. Yet now he is equally at home with high-ranking officers of the police force and notable Sicilians in exile, and none of his commuted sentences were for a lesser term than fifteen years. His Money-Making Schemes are legendary, even among those who can convert a fiver to five grand without stirring from the Turkish Bath. His example has been often in my mind.

A *Fourth*, and final, *Financial Fallacy* is easily exploded. This is that Great Wealth quickly begins to pall: that tastes glutted with smoked salmon and paté de fois gras soon long again for wholemeal bread and lentil potage. Oddly enough, this is a myth put about by the Poor crazed from eating too many lentils. My own experience is that while Enough is as good as a Feast, one can soon have enough of Enough, and everybody knows that smoked salmon is the best accompaniment to wholemeal bread.

It is not possible to pretend that the Rich escape such blows of fate as cancer or death, although they will be the first to know when immortality becomes practical. It is just that the rich agenda of life has many more items on it than that of the Poor, particularly under 'Any Other Business'. My intention is not merely to fatten the wallet, but to open a door into those extra items, allowing You to enjoy the same privileges as the successful composer of 'Viva España', and the inventor of the plastic bag.

THE MASTERS APPROACH TO GREAT WEALTH

I have condensed the art of money-making into a few simple rules, which are the general principles underlying the most complicated deals. These should be taken to heart, because the operation of the schemes themselves depends on a grasp of these essentials, the same way Euclid had to define a straight line before he could start doing complicated things with cubes. What we are seeking is the shortest distance between Poverty and Wealth; many would-be entrepreneurs spend their whole lives stuck on some hypotenuse or other.

1 IDENTIFY DEMAND AND SUPPLY IT

People want things: this is as much an essential part of *Homo graspens* as the need to eat and drink and find a good accountant. The medium of exchange between thing and buyer is money, which comes in the form of bundles of used notes. The purchaser is usually a *worker*, one who toils at tasks to save up bundles of money to buy things, while the person (or persons) who manufactures the thing is *another* worker, one who toils endlessly in the manufacture of things for other workers to toil endlessly to buy. The person in the well-cut suit with the leather attaché-case who brings the labours of these two together is YOU. Your role is to walk away with most of the medium of exchange.

Corollary: *The Water Bed Syndrome.* The extension of this process leads to the invention of things that people *do not yet know they want*. This is the field for the truly creative schemer, and it is musing upon such imponderables that we maestros of manufacture spend apparently motionless afternoons drifting about on yachts in the Aegean. This creative process is named after the water bed, the perfect example, because people had been getting on perfectly well without beds filled with water for hundreds of years, apart from the occasional accident. Yet once it had been invented it sold with a briskness matched only by electric toothbrushes and digital toasters.

2 THERE IS ROOM TO BE RICH

Anyone who has tried to cross Knightsbridge on Friday at 4 in the afternoon might have thought that there was already a saturation of large cars driven by workers in peaked caps. Fortunately, this is not the case. The more Rich there are the more possibilities they create for more Rich. For example, the Rich have time to reflect on the

Higher things of Life, to question their Inner Values, and to keep their weight down. The commodity value of Truth, Beauty and Enlightenment is pretty high on that Other Stock Market for which there is no Quotation. *This is one of the quickest ways to get your own worker with a peaked cap.* I am convinced that the number of Rich can increase indefinitely.*

Corollary: *The eternal triangle.* This law of economics says that a triangle always has its narrowest point uppermost, i.e. that the Poor at the bottom will always outnumber the Rich at the top. However, by turning the triangle upside down you can have a lot more Rich at the top and a lot less Poor at the bottom, which is a very simple thing to do. This is known as lateral thinking.

3 SOMEBODY ALWAYS GETS THE SHORT STRAW

This is very true. In any transaction involving much shuffling about of the medium of exchange one of the parties usually finishes up worse off. This is a law of the Universe known as *Entropy*, which means that not everybody can be on the up-and-up at the same time, and somebody has got to go to the wall. Viewing this as part of a universal process, one can see that this is as inevitable as the world turning, water running downhill, or second-hand Fords needing a rebore. Usually the character that gets the short straw deserves it anyway. Many years of experience have proved to me that these unfortunates are short in stature with perpetually running eyes and a tendency to give money to importuning strangers. They are not to be trusted with money at the best of times, and it really is a kindness to remove it from them.

Corollary: *Cash as cash can.* Using logic and flair it follows that those who succeed in their money-making schemes *deserve* it. Love is one of the Higher Human Emotions, and those who feel truly affectionate towards deposit bags brimming with pristine fivers *deserve* to have their love returned. Nothing should come between a man and his money: what enterprise has joined together let no man put asunder, unless he is paying interest considerably over the odds.

A helpful hint for peace of mind. In spite of the impeccable logic of the foregoing I know beginners sometimes have difficulty getting to sleep

* The widespread urge for Upwards Mobility is revealed scientifically in a recent **MASTERPLAN** poll. When asked, 'Would you rather be: (a) grindingly poor or (b) extremely rich?', 96.6 per cent of those sampled opted for (b). The 3.3 per cent were Don't Knows (0.1 per cent was a Mr W. C. Bindweed).

from thinking about small men with watery eyes giving away money to hard-pressed widows. Try putting a handful or two of new tenners into the pillowcase; as you toss and turn you will find they produce a delightful rustling sound, more soothing than 'Max Jaffa's Honeymoon Medley'. It is the sound of your money returning your affection, sweet somethings whispering of higher interest rates to come, fresh yields and debentures new.

4 SPREAD YOUR IRONS IN THE FIRE

Many a budding entrepreneur has put all his eggs in one basket, and they have refused to hatch, so that he is left with egg on his face. This is very unwise. The rule to follow is: keep your fingers in as many pies as possible. A Great Schemer is able to keep a huge number of balls in the air at the same time without putting his foot in it. I myself have an almost infinite variety of different enterprises on the go at once, so many indeed that the whole *Weltanschauung* is only apparent to me, and that only for a few seconds at a time. Remember, the human brain is an organ of almost unimaginable complexity which nobody understands, being full of grey, wobbly stuff with plenty of room to hide ideas of one kind or another. Ledgers, on the other hand, are just an open book.

I find it useful never to write anything down. This is because things change so fast if you have a full stable of lively horses that you never know which chickens are going to come home to roost. Also, books are very difficult to burn in a hurry.

Corollary: *The invisible man.* Once you have an enormous number of deals on the boil it is possible to move money around from one deal to the next. You become the invisible man, plucking out a thousand here, a thousand there, from the frantic whirlpool of circulating assets. Nobody but you knows where the cash came from, and nobody but you knows where it goes to, and sometimes even you will have your doubts. I have been carrying a cheque around in my wallet for several months from one W. C. Bindweed made out to the Masters Monetary Miasma Company Ltd; I have never heard of Bindweed, and the company is not familiar to me either.

NUTSHELL SUMMARY OF THE MASTERS APPROACH

- Seek a Demand and find a Supply. If you cannot find a Demand invent one; if you cannot find a Supply commission one; buy an attaché case.

- There is plenty of room at the Top; it is only a question of finding your way through the Middle. Buy a sauna.

- Do not worry about the little man with the eyes full of tears; he *likes* giving his money away, and you deserve to have it. Buy peace of mind.

- Diversify, diversify. The quickest way through a maze is to build it yourself. Trust your brain, and always keep it by your side.

The Schemes which form the later part of this book are the lines of attack drawn up from this plan of campaign. The world is a vast storehouse of riches; enterprise and flair will make sure you get *your* share, which is rather more than most people's.

A note on names. It is a curious fact that people with names like Eric Normal or Pam Grebe never seem to be enormously rich. Rich people have names like Nubar Gulbenkian or Aristotle Onassis or Roderick Masters. Fortunately, names are easy to change, but make sure you choose the *right* one.* For example:

Before		After	
	Sid Griddle		Nubar Onassis
	Mavis Crump		Fiona Fforbes-Golightly
	Zbigniew Przbrezelzzski		Garth Fortune
	Walter Wilter		Clint Thrust
	O. D. Smith		S. O. Bigge

CREATING THE IMAGE

Everybody needs an image, and for those with genuine pecuniary motivation, this is doubly important. It is amazing how highly lucrative deals always finish up in the direction of those who look as if they are used to handling highly lucrative deals. Persons with the right image give off an impalpable *aura*. For example, it is not unusual

* There is plenty of scope for imagination here. The name **Roderick Masters** is protected by patent No. 34878381 for use by Money-Making Schemes Inc. and any infringement will result in appropriate action being taken.

for *complete strangers* to rush up to me in the street to offer me a piece of the latest deal in Go-go dancers to Qatar or exotic lingerie by post. Yet this is not a matter of inbuilt *savoir faire*, but rather a skill of presentation learned and practised in the privacy of my Esher *pied-à-terre* away from the hurly-burly of the international money market. Fortunately, I can pass on some of the secrets to my readers: there is no reason why YOU should not become one of those to whom wheeling and dealing looks like second nature, particularly if it comes naturally to you.

The office. This is the place where deals are clinched and discreet paper packages are exchanged. An office should be as empty as possible. Cluttered offices look as if they are dedicated to hard work rather than high profit. I usually have a few big plants around. A large desk is essential. You place your telephones on the desk, and a variety of recording instruments inside it. You have an appointments diary on the desk too, although you do not use it much because you are hardly ever in the office except when you wish to use the variety of recording instruments.

'MONEY IS THE ROOT OF ALL INVESTMENT' R.M.

The regular inhabitant of the office is the *personal assistant*, whose job it is to answer the telephone to say that you are in the Bahamas. Your personal assistant is a young lady, but not less than twenty-five, who looks especially good sucking a Parker Executive. Personal assistants come in two varieties: the *absolutely stunning* and the *enormously attractive*. The former is a useful distraction when it comes to your client reading the finer details in the small print, but they have been known to interfere with the smooth running of the financial brain, and in general I would opt for the latter. The personal assistant should buff up the desk at frequent intervals, and should always sit with her legs crossed with a notepad resting on her sheer nylons. She will have to know the names of the actors in your financial drama, but she should never be told the plot, let alone the punchlines. Once in a while you may get an assistant who *knows too much*. This can be dangerous, as it may result in the threat of defection to a third party who may profit from the said knowledge. There are only two ways out of such an *impasse*: a clean break (often with unwanted financial repercussions) or *matrimony*. The second Mrs Jarvis (now Lady M*****) rose to that position because of her knowledge of what came to be known as the Cardboard Cornflakes Scandal. My friend Jarvis emerged from what could have been a *débâcle* hardly more tarnished than he was before, thanks to a sympathetic judge in Reno and a two-week honeymoon special in the Blisserama, Acapulco. Even today he cannot bear the sight of cornflakes.

Personal demeanour. A smile costs nothing. A continuous smile always seems to have a remarkable effect on your opposite numbers, and after half an hour or so they are always anxious to complete the business. A firm handshake is also a valuable *sine qua non*. This is done by grasping the proffered hand neatly and cleanly and giving it a short waggle, while maintaining eye-to-eye contact and your smile. NEVER hang on too long or this may give your opposite number the upper hand.

Always call your dealerees 'Mr X' if they are not as rich as you are; if they are richer call them 'Bill'. If they are American call them 'Sir'. The aim is to make them feel *privileged* to know you, which is something that comes easily in my case. Never mention the subject of money at first, but indulge in idle chit-chat about well-known persons like Shirley Bassey or Michael Parkinson that you have met at the Mouchoir Blessé and similar watering spots. Swap anecdotes about the best time to holiday in the Outer Antilles. Your tone should encourage confidences, and leaks about possible take-over bids. I have perfected a deep chuckle, which I learned during a spell as Father Christmas when the Schemes were suffering a temporary eclipse. Yet always have a slight *frisson* of mystery, as if you are only telling a small part of what you really know. Never sell yourself short – you will regret it for a long time if you do. And through your smile be ever alert to the subtle hint, the *nuance*, which may reveal loot for the picking. Remember: the manner makes the Man makes the Money.

The suit. This is the uniform of Financial Man. It comes as a jacket for keeping credit cards in, trousers for walking around in, and a waistcoat for filling the gap between the other two. Choice of a suit is very important – it is the first thing your potential deal will see. Your suit should *suit* you. My own preference is for tweed, which carries with it a sniff of the grouse moor, and does not crumple too badly on the overnight hop across the Atlantic. I have a matching hat with a few salmon flies in for outdoor assignations. But you must fit your material to your *own* personality; some, I know, prefer stripes to dog-tooth, but I find that I pull off very few *coups* with dark grey men.

The tie. This is a complex signalling device which hooks around the neck and under the shirt by means of a special knot. I would recommend the variety known as Old School because (a) it does you good if it is recognised and (b) it does not do any harm if it is *not* recognised. Ties with mermaids on should be avoided. Selection of prestigious models available from: *The House Masters'*, P.O. Box 53, Birmingham 24. Ties can be dispensed with when chasing a deal in Cannes or Monaco; substitute a cravat. Old school cravats are supplied by the same reliable manufacturers.

Shirts. Avoid dark purple ones as these are worn by interior designers, and dark green ones, as these are worn by university lecturers and similar undesirables.

Extras. A buttonhole can be a stylish extra. I am against jewellery in general, but a chunky piece of gold or diamond can inspire confidence.

> 'LOOK AFTER THE PENNIES AND THE BALANCE SHEETS WILL LOOK RESPECTABLE ENOUGH TO LOOK AFTER THEMSELVES' R.M.

Rendezvouses. Very few of the biggest deals are clinched in the office. Instead I recommend the more intimate atmosphere of a rendezvous, where schemer can meet with schemer to get down to the nitty-gritty. The cocktail bars of International Hotels are one of my favoured venues. These have the advantage that they are the same in Tahiti or Taiwan, Tunbridge Wells or Torremolinos, so that you never feel you need any luggage other than the dollar. The smoky glass accoutrements and low-slung seats in luxurious dralonette induce an appropriate feeling of well-being, and I find the gentle buzz of neighbouring conversations about money promotes a sense of the proper order of things. Also, all taxi drivers will drive you straight to the Hilton at the first wave of a hefty bunch of *escudos*. Never drink more than two cocktails, but you can eat as many of those little potato worms as you like.

Or you can go to a private club, like the 'Nitty Gritty'. Here you are on first name terms with everybody, which puts you at an advantage, especially if you cut the barman in on that export deal of defective panti-hose to Alma-Ata. He will mix, for your guest, the celebrated Deal Clincher, a concoction that always renders the drinker reckless before speechless.

I know there are some who like to go to gambling clubs. The

atmosphere of red plush *does* sometimes induce a financially favourable *frisson*, and the clatter of enormously valuable chips has a musical quality reminiscent of Fernando Hubris and his Latin-American Seven. I would recommend this rendezvous only when you have a large number of slightly tacky notes to dispose of, because there is always the danger that your dealeree might be tempted to direct his money towards the management of the club rather than to you.

Money-making hint here. Always tip barmen generously, at least if you think they will recognise you again. A disgruntled barman can clear his throat in a way that makes weeks of work on your smile and handshake superfluous. He may even spill *crème de menthe* on your tweeds, which means you will have to take your suit rather than your client to the cleaners. A folded fiver on the till will often yield an hundredfold, that is until something goes wrong with the Alma-Ata panti-hose project.

Dress. There is more to clothes than keeping draughts off your torso. Your apparel is the outward show of that Inward Drive to Riches: the Mind is tailor to the Man. You cannot get to Mayfair in a Parka and Hush Puppies. Of course once you are enormously rich you can turn up at Claridge's in a purple loincloth and they will step up the heating for you – that kind of cash will probably start a trend in any case. But for those on the up-and-up the message is: it is smart to be smart.

Shoes. These are not just stiff bits of leather to keep your feet dry. Shoes should be clean and shiny, and avoid that embarrassing squeak that can interrupt the *dénouement* of the big deal. The Italians make very good shoes, probably because they are used to being quick on their feet. Avoid green shoes.

THE WORD GAME

One of the signs of the true entrepreneur is a mastery of the language of the big deal. Every sphere of money-making has its own words, and this may intimidate the uninitiated. But **do not be fooled**, these special words are just cooked up by the Rich to conceal the fact that the making of money is a remarkably simple process. From time to time in this book I will present straightforward explanations of the technical terms used to make things sound more difficult than they are. Remember, the acquisition of great wealth is a matter of having the right *attitude* to the right *opportunity*, and never grumbling into the telephone.

Once you have mastered such technical terms the strange fact is that you can actually *drop* them again. This is a characteristic of the highest echelons of International Finance, where the more important the deal the less is said, because of the dangers of anybody over-hearing. The language is entirely that of innuendo and *je ne sais quois*:

Mr A: 'Mr Finkelstein, I am in communication about the *matter of our deep, mutual concern.*'

Mr B: 'Please call me Mr B, Mr Bigge. With regard to the *subject under consideration* I am assured by *certain parties* that we may bring our *joint interests* to a speedy and *mutually satisfactory conclusion.*'

Mr A: 'That is entirely as it should be, Mr B, and, please, do call me A. And am I to take it that the movement of the *specified commodity* is *via the usual channels*?'

Mr B: 'And in the capable hands of *an old and trusted friend*, Mr A.'

Mr A: 'I am glad to hear it, Mr B. No doubt I should confirm that completion of the *undertaking* will be *acknowledged in the appropriate way.*'

Mr B: 'Naturally, Mr A. A *person not unfamiliar to both of us* will ensure that all goes *according to plan.* I do not anticipate any interference from a *third party of our acquaintance*, but just in case I have taken the *necessary precautions.*'

Mr A: 'Prudent as always, Mr B. I am sure we can expect further enterprises which will be *not entirely unrewarding* to both of us in the *none too distant future.* And please give my best to Mrs B and the little bs.'

Mr B: 'And to Mrs A. One last thing. . . .'

Mr A: 'Certainly, Mr B.'

Mr B: 'Single denomination notes this time.'

Mr A: 'Taken as read, Mr B.'

Skilled practitioners in the art can carry on in this vein for hours without giving anything away. The conversation is incomprehensible to any third party listening in with a Sophisticated Electronic Device. It could refer equally well to moving diamonds from Jo'burg to Miami, or ball bearings from Burslem to Llandrindod Wells. Occasionally even A and B get somewhat confused over the meaning of innuendos, especially if they are unsure which of several A's or B's they are talking to.

RAISING A LOAN

Most deals are floated on credit, sustained on tick, and brought off in the nick of time. It is essential to be able to get hold of large chunks of cash with no strings attached while you negotiate the delicate middle stretch of making a fortune. You have probably noticed that *banks* are normally pretty flush with high denomination notes, and most of these the public never get to see at all. To get your hands on some of this cash so as to turn a lively percentage you generally have to see the Bank Manager. Do not be alarmed: it is only a question of *know your Manager*.

Bank Managers come in two varieties:

- A thin little man in a dark grey suit with a mouth puckered into a tube from many years of saying, **'No'**. He regards all the money in the bank as his own, and is called Mr Blenkinsop.

- A big man in a green sports jacket with elbow pads, who will accept a couple of large doubles at the golf club, where he spends most of his time. He is called Mr Haugh-Handley, and only went into the bank because his father was on the board before the war. **Only deal with managers of the second type.**

They have a touching belief that money is intended for distribution among their friends. Your aim is to become one of their intimate circle, swap trout flies on the verdant banks of the River Trundle, and take them for as much as you can. I often find that allowing them regular strolls around the rhododendrons with your personal assistant helps to loosen the purse-strings. The golden rule of borrowing is: credit does you credit. Once you have landed the first big loan, subsequent ones are no problem. Nowadays I find it very difficult to leave a bank without a large personal cheque, and more than once I have had a fistful of them. I have to spend days thereafter working out what to do with the money.

Loan sharks are another source of revenue. But these are usually men with firm handshakes and tweed suits who are out to make as much money as quickly as they can with absolutely no effort whatsoever. Not recommended.*

---

* There are some exceptions to this. If you *do* need this service, try:
 Masterloan Ltd,
  Lot's Mansions,
   Gradgrind Street,
    London WC3 9GH.

THE MASTERS MEMORANDUM

● You *can* become rich with a minimum of effort: commit yourself to it.

● Master the language of money. Seek out opportunities. *Create* opportunities. Never scowl in the office.

● Take credit for what you have done, and reinvest it double quick through your External Account.

● Money-making is an exciting journey across the Sea of Enterprise. Make sure it is YOU with your hand at the helm, not in the hold with a couple of duff fivers.

HOW
TO BECOME EXTREMELY
RICH
FROM THE POOR AND
VULNERABLE

The poor are defined as those lacking any money, and the vulnerable are those who cannot look after it when they have it.

There have always been poor. The Bible is full of examples of people without two brass farthings to rub together, and plenty of these were smitten with sore boils as well. It is a Law of Nature that any heap has to have a bottom; and a quick examination of heaps in farmyards will show you that some of the creatures living in the lower regions are fairly unprepossessing. Equally, it is a Law of Nature that Birds of Paradise feed on worms and other lowly crustaceans, because the Well-endowed inevitably prey upon the Spineless and Crawling, which is why they were put there in the first place. It is exactly the same with people.

C. Darwin first noticed this important fact about the behaviour of animals from many hours spent watching the behaviour of his Beagle. He called it the Survival of the Fittest. As far as money is concerned this means that the Schemer has a duty to acquire as much

15

as he can from the Poor and Vulnerable, because only in this way will they eventually be eliminated. When my friend Jarvis sent the least affluent members of his family off to labour in a Bolivian tin mine he was rightly congratulated by several Members of his Club for the contribution he had made towards the improvement of the species. But a **WORD OF WARNING** here. It sometimes happens that even the most ambidextrous of entrepreneurs suffers a temporary eclipse that puts them back at the bottom of the heap. These should not be confused with the *real* poor. Indeed, after the unlucky Affair of the Inflammable Fire Escapes even I was forced to renew my acquaintance with lumpy mattresses in rooms hired by the day. But such passing unfortunates can be easily recognised by their air of optimism, their *sang froid,* and by the speed with which they get loans from the Poor surrounding them.

Even the poorest Poor cherish a notion that Things are going to get better. For this reason they scrimp their few spare notes together, and are always vigilant for methods of turning this small pile into a Gargantuan one. The promise of moderate affluence will not be enough – the comfortable semi with the second-hand Cortina gracing the drive. No, only instant and enormous wealth will be a sufficient bait, enough to banish Army Surplus Stores and flaccid chips from yesterday's *Sun* to the realms of a bad dream. YOU can offer this chance. It does not matter if the chance is 100,000,000 to one against, it is only necessary that it should exist. Even by providing Hope in the midst òf Want you are decreasing the sum of Human Misery, and this is one of the pleasantest ways to earn your place at one of the plusher hotels in the Scilly Isles.

There are numerous ways of dangling the dream of great wealth before the Poor, e.g.:

You are privy to a secret deal in the upper *echelons* of High Finance, which is explicable only in terms of 4 per cent debentures, preferred issues, and the take-over of Motorised Universal Stores Executives (MOUSE) by Rotating Amalgamated Traders (RAT), which the Poor will not understand. Guaranteed return on £50 is £50,000 on condition the rice crop in Bali does not fail. It does.

Simple competition. Remember, the football pools were invented in a back room in Grimsby which has since been demolished. It is important that the competition can be solved by writing a simple cross, because many of the Poor can only remember this letter of the alphabet. 'Spot the ball' competitions are a good money spinner, in which the punter has to mark with a cross the position of a football (invisible) on a photograph showing various surprised-looking players who are peering this way and that. The most profitable version of

16

this is when the ball has gone off the picture and into the crowd, which is why the players are looking surprised.

Put a moderate-sized advertisement in the newspaper with the wording: 'Send only £5 to find the secret of how I changed £5 into £50,000' with some additional stuff in words of one syllable about how simple the method is, and how it can be done by anybody with £5. To all who post you £5 send back a duplicated letter instructing them to place an advertisement in the newspaper with the words 'Send only £5 to find the secret of how I changed £5 into £50,000.' Move monthly.

CHARITY BEGINS AT HOME

Everybody needs somewhere to lay his head after a hard day, preferably a bed. The best place to keep a bed is in some kind of room, and this accounts for the widespread use of rooms for living in. The Poor are often short of a room, because of general fecklessness, and because they are always moving about trying to improve their lot. YOU supply the accommodation in your less salubrious properties, which you picked up for a song because they were in danger of falling into the canal behind, probably as a result of the articulated lorries passing the front door, airplanes skimming the roof, and the concerted movement of rats. You charge a lot because of the likely demise of your investment. (You can also make quite a bit extra from giving permission to the BBC to make documentary films there on the Problems of the Poor.)

Occasionally it happens that one of your tenants is a little slow in coming up with the £50 rent which is rightfully yours. This can be a problem, and here I suggest you send around one of your friends with scars to put in a word of persuasion.* Persistent non-payers can usually be induced to move if the floor is taken out. Persons of alien ethnic origin are highly suitable tenants because they can be moved in on day and night shifts and they cannot pronounce the word 'intimidation'. People from Naples feel particularly at home. In general I would avoid old persons because they are not likely to survive the collapse of a staircase. They also tend to be visited by organis-

---

* An International service of the right kind of friends is provided by:
  Der Masterrace,
    Schweinstrs. 45,
      Bütingen-am-Groin,
        FDR.

ations like Meals on Wheels and Oxfam who might dispute your right to supply this valuable social need for accommodation. You can, however, house people sent by the local council, who have nowhere else to go. This will also guarantee that you will not be knocked down, except by accident, when you can claim heftily on the insurance.

One small hint: never call in person at your properties. The sight of your Astrakhan coat and plum-coloured XJ6 seems to irritate tenants, and the price of a respray these days is pure exploitation.

HELP FOR THOSE IN NEED

This is a useful way to combine a sense of serving the community with a regular source of income. You must found a *charity*, to be supported by donations from the Rich and Guilty. To do this you need the patronage of an aristocratic personage who is not averse to a few weeks a year in your Venezuelan vineyard. Irish peers, and especially Lord Feargus of Casheen, are often willing to lend their names to these ventures. In practice there are already numerous charities catering for the obvious Needy, like impotent tom-cats or veterans of the Wars of the Roses. I have found that the most profitable charitable organisations are of a highly *specialised* nature. My own Society for The Sustenance and Education of Divorced Nuns has been doing very nicely for a number of years, and I have travelled all over the world in an attempt to find a worthy recipient. Administrative expenses consume a certain proportion of the interest, and we have built a well-equipped *résidence* a few miles to the north of Grasse which will one day house our Needy. At present it is occupied by the housekeeper, Mlle Claudette Volupté.

> 'MONEY OILS THE WHEELS; OIL MONEY WHEELS THE DEALS' R.M.

Another kind of Charity is that concerned with the promulgation and furtherance of knowledge, the kind of organisation for which I feel a particular personal sympathy. It is some five years since I founded the Institute for Internal Revenue Studies and the regular publication of our organ, the *Journal of Evasion*, has probably given more pleasure to entrepreneurs with a philosophical turn of mind than anything since the reduction in the top rate of income tax. The number of members of the Institute is growing continuously, and it is a measure of the International Esteem in which our journal is held that we now attract subscriptions from gauchos in Argentina, and pearl-gatherers in the Cayman Islands. Membership is open to all those with an interest in matters fiscal, and they can enjoy the privilege of browsing through Learned Journals such as the *Proceedings of the Yorkshire Muck and Brass Society* in our Park Lane library, without fear of being harassed by officials seeking access to their ledgers.

But it is the Poorest who are the Neediest. There are many who lack the wherewithal for even the most lowly accommodation, whose life is measured out in gills of meths and bread too tough for the attrition of pigeons. Charities such as St Crippen's Trust care for such unwanted human dross. The wealthy and responsible citizens of Hampstead and similar desirable areas are happy to subscribe to such a cause, because they do not like the sight of very scruffy persons rifling through their dustbins for bits of gristle. The charity provides beds which are regularly fumigated, and nourishing soup, full of the goodness of gravy browning. The profit comes from the numerous television appearances you are required to make as Spokesman for those who have no spokesman. With luck, you can spend so much time travelling around appearing on chat shows, and eating out with Important Persons with an interest in the plight of the Poorest in Society, that you need never go near St Crippen's headquarters at Rillington House at all. In any case, the conversation of the Poorest tends to be very dull, being mostly confined to vaguely musical mumblings about how they belong to Glasgow.

TOIL, SWEAT AND TEARS

There is an inexplicable instinct among many of the Poor to work hard. Possibly this arises from the mistaken idea that hard work will produce affluence, but more probably it has become ingrained in the system from many generations of labour in grimy pits. This love of work seems to apply particularly to those born outside our own shores, e.g. Pakistan, and no doubt this is a tribute to the nutritive powers of rice. Whatever the cause, many such diligent persons, fired with enthusiasm for labour of the dullest kind, find themselves without the pernickety official permission to pursue their labourings. This is where the ingenuity and generosity of the entrepreneur comes in. YOU will provide a premises, hidden in the tortuous byways of one of the less-respectable suburbs, where many of these frustrated types can gather together under one roof to spend unnumbered happy hours bent over a sewing machine. Not only will these people then have the satisfaction of sating their inexhaustible urge to work, but they will also be able to chat away happily in Gujerati, which is easier here than in the checkout in Woolworth's. The rate of payment for such labour is very low because it is as much pleasure as work, and they can always make up the total by working fifteen hours at a stretch. The dexterity of such workpersons is a delight to behold, and they seem to have a natural knack for the manufacture of Exclusive Paris Designs, which you can then sell off in the King's Road at Maison Maître, and similar exclusive *couturiers*.

You should avoid cramming *too* many of these workers together under one roof, especially if they are working on such highly incendiary materials as Flammulon.® My friend Jarvis barely managed to extricate himself from the affair that came to be known as the Black Hole of East Ham by virtue of the quick adoption of the Bolivian nationality which he retained for several years. I generally appoint one of the workforce as an overseer, with an incentive bonus of 3p an hour. This man often meets officials from the Department of Immigration. He usually goes off to Wormwood Scrubs happy in the knowledge that his large family will be able to keep body and soul together by their continued diligence while he is away. Even if he is unhappy, all he knows is that your name is 'Mr Smith' (unless, that is, your name is Smith, when you are known as Mr Jones).

THE HEART OF GOLD

The human heart is an organ situated just underneath the chest, noted for its incessant thumping. Of all parts of the anatomy it appears to be the most vulnerable. I have seen cases of entrepreneurs famous for their *legerdemain* rendered temporarily inept because of infections lodged in this small bit of tissue, even to the extent of turning down foolproof chances of doubling their Swiss currency on deposit. It is no surprise that the heart can be a source of income. Some Heart Specialists of my acquaintance seem to spend more time on Cap Ferrat than any other type of Schemer. Either sex may apply themselves to this task, although a certain physical symmetry is undoubtedly an advantage. Remarkably little effort is essential, apart from occasional bouts of exercise of an intimate nature. The object is to entrap the heart of a Vulnerable person who is also the major shareholder of Consolidated Assets Inc. A few classes of persons are particularly likely to be Vulnerable:

- **Widows**. These have rich, dead husbands. They usually wear weeds, and carry large bottles of gin around in their handbags. They secretly yearn to splash around some of their assets. *You* show them how evenings spent in the Clochard Enchainé and days cruising around Antibes in large boats provide the best way to assuage their grief. A Good Time always makes death seem a thing of the past.

- **Widowers**. As widows, but with dead wives, and whisky. Conspicuous purchases of furs and diamonds help to ease the burden of Loss. Teach them that there is nothing like a generous Present to bury the Past.

- **Confirmed bachelors**. Difficult types usually interested only in the classification of small, green beetles or Samoan postage stamps issued in 1923. Swot up on coleoptera and Samoan franking methods, which will help your conquest. Then it is your task to persuade the *enamoratus* that the best place to study small, green beetles is aboard a well-appointed yacht cruising around Antibes. Women generally stand a better chance with these.

- **Ugly**. People with huge noses or ears like scallops are very Vulnerable. Remember, you never judge a bank by its counter, only by what it has in its vaults. Keep your sights fixed on the Deeper Assets, or if you find this impossibly difficult wear dark glasses with funny lenses.

In general I would advise avoiding marriage. Marriage is the only contract to add Family In-Law's to the debit column, and it can be tricky to escape from. It is the only deal in which you have to see the client every day before breakfast. The liberal doling-out of assets often seems to stop shortly after the knot has been tied, and legal partners can start demanding to know the details of some of your more *recherché* schemes, which have hitherto been secrets shared only between you and the Financial Brain.

MARRYING MONEY

The Vulnerable are usually particularly anxious to be wed. This is because of a belief that hitching up with the perfect partner will halve life's problems rather than double them, which is what always happens. While *direct* participation in this misconception is invariably a disaster for the money-maker who wants to keep both hands on the purse strings, the role of middleman is, as always, a favourable one. You become the medium for two Vulnerables to meet and mate, for which you charge a fee that guarantees that matrimonial commitment will not be taken lightly. Acceptable names for such agencies are:

The
Successful Professional's Matrimonial Agency

THE
BETTER OFF PERSON'S COMPATIBILITY COMPANY

Cupid's Bower (Over 40s) Inc.

*Adèle Rothschild-Fauntleroy's
Friendship Services*

No money is to be made out of mating the Poor, who have plenty of chances to meet in the pawnshop. My own exclusive bureau, Mastermate *(No Paupers)* Ltd, has been responsible for the splicing of many lonely Vulnerables, 85 per cent of whom were still married after one month. The office is in the usual tones of tasteful green, decked with pictures of famous partnerships, like Franklin and Eleanor Roosevelt, and Joe and Mama Fats Gumboilioni. In the back room you house your computer, which objectively sifts the qualities of your various clients to ensure complete compatibility. I use two cardboard boxes labelled 'Men' and 'Women'. For some of your clients with Special Tastes you do not even have to riffle through the second box.

RÉSUMÉ

- Poverty is the cheapest route to Riches.

- Everybody needs four walls and a ceiling; the very poor can dispense with the ceiling.

- Charity is the best way to turn Giving into living.

- Hard work and long hours provide the answer for keeping the Poor out of the ghetto – at least between midnight and 6 a.m.

HOW TO BECOME EXTREMELY RICH FROM
THE POOR AND VULNERABLE

● Always look out for those who cannot look out for themselves.

● Avoid marriage; it is the only contract without an escape clause in the small print.

● It is never a waste of time spending time on people who spend money on you.

● Two Vulnerables can make a marriage; four can make a Marriage Bureau.

HOW TO ACHIEVE
INSTANT AND GARGANTUAN
WEALTH
FROM POPULAR MUSIC

Music has been part of human culture ever since Orpheus and the Lutes formed the first Group. Nowadays, it is one of the quickest routes to the top, and many of my close acquaintances on the Côte D'Azur still sport the quiffs and needle marks that rocketed them into unusual affluence. Not that I am referring to concertos and symphonies and string trios; although there is good money to be made in this kind of performance it has to be said that you need a bit of practice to be able to do all the twiddly bits with your fingers, and very few entrepreneurs worth the name have time for that sort of thing.

The Big Money comes from hitting the style and trend of the times, giving the young people a meaningful and relevant message with which to interpret their own lives, and charging them a lot for getting in to the Shrines to worship their Idols. I am *not* suggesting that you yourself should try to be one of these idols. These have a generally tiring time, rushing all over the world screaming at people and looking bad-tempered on the television; they often finish up 'freaked out' by the time they are twenty-one, which means that they go off into the Cotswolds to become prematurely senile. No, rather you should be the manager, confidant and moulder of the idols, and the one with 20 per cent of the takings to 2 per cent of the effort.

The world is full of young persons who wish to make it big in the world of popular music. It is your role to fulfil their dreams. What better way to considerable affluence than to propel some youth with a bad complexion from the poor end of Nottingham to international stardom, a white Rolls Royce and expensive stimulants? It may even help his complexion! Of course, it is the fate of many of those young stars to burn out as quickly as they have risen from obscurity, but there are always dozens more queueing up.

THE GROUP

The group is the unit of currency in the pop trade. It consists of a few people to hold guitars, one to sit behind a drum kit, and a lead singer, who is the one with a personality. The time was when groups had names like The Harmonics or The Mellotone Sisters. This will not produce the right *ambience* today; here are some acceptable names for groups:

These names are easier to remember than Perry Starborgling and His Intergalactic Three. If success does not come with one name you can easily change to another. Failure dogged my own group, The

Tingling Sensations, until I changed their name to **500-VOLT SHOCK**, which sent them straight into the charts.

Once you have a group it is necessary to get them to supply music, which is called *sound* in the trade. Unfortunately, the most market-able kinds of sound change every three weeks or so, so you have to keep a pretty keen eye on the charts to see what is in favour at the time. One of my most talented Combos, The Chameleons, were able to change their musical style at the drop of a semitone. On the other hand, there is a good market in *revivals*, which means redoing some-thing that has already been done, only worse, to cash in on the nostalgia that fifteen-year-olds feel for when they were thirteen. Sometimes if you are a bit slow catching up with a New Sound it can finish up making money as a Revival.

Things change so fast that it is a good idea to send somebody to find the *avant-garde*. These groups usually hang around in dingy cellars, pursued by a fanatical band of devotees dressed in flour-bags. Do not be put off: they are the hit men of tomorrow. They are usually so delighted about being discovered that they will sign the contract paying you 75 per cent of their earnings. For the first few months this only amounts to £5 a week, but once their sound is discovered you should be coining thousands. By the time they have made enough to employ a lawyer to winkle them out of their contract (more £000's for you) they are usually *passé*, and all they can do then is to hang around hoping to strike lucky in the two-year nos-talgia boom.

Most sounds have already been thought of, but the relentless search for the New Sound goes on. My own latest innovations, revealed in advance exclusively to readers of this book and released on the Masters' Voice label, include:*

The Monotones. Sensational 12-piece band of musicians who sing the word 'paint stripper' *entirely on one note*. 'Deep expression of contemporary alienation' – *New Musical Express*. Sexually provocative 'b' side identical, but omits the word 'paint'.

The Bats. Diminutive vocalists producing entirely new sound beyond the range of human hearing. The first attempt to cash in on the lucrative doggy market. 'A meaningful comment on the Human Condition.' *Hound and Horse*.

Digestive Tract. Exciting new group with the amplified alimentary sound. First album 'Prawn Curry' shortly to be released. 'Profound

* ©Music Masters Ltd,
  'Molto Vivace',
    Slag End Ind. Estate,
    Wormsley.

insight into the working of the rectal muscles.' *British Medical Journal.*

THE LYRIC

Most songs are sung to words, which are known as the *lyric*. There is still a reasonably good market in songs dealing with bluebirds and happy memories of loved ones temporarily parted, but a generally tougher line is favoured by the young, dealing with such matters as the pointlessness of life and how to slit a jugular vein. The simple lyrics of the new generation have a stark simplicity appropriate to the age of the automatic coffee vendor. Unfortunately, this means that many of the old rhyming stand-bys have become obsolete, and a new set of rhymes has evolved to take their place. To help you with the concoction of lyrics for your groups, here are some of the old favourites with their new equivalents:

'Feeling blue' used to rhyme with *'over you'*, now rhymes with *'sniffin' glue'*.

'September' always used to rhyme with *'remember'*, now rhymes with *'dismember'*.

'Love' traditionally rhymed with *'heavens above'*, but now goes with *'push and shove'*.

'Over you' used to rhyme with *'ever true'*, but now rhymes with *'wanna screw'*.

'Sparkling eyes' always went with *'sunny skies'*, but now goes with *'other guys'*.

'Life' used to rhyme with *'wife'*, now rhymes with *'knife'*.

'Heart' used to rhyme with *'never part'*, now rhymes with *'Exchange and Mart'*.

'Hope' used to couple with *'elope'*, but now goes with *'dope'*.

One of my own stable, Deathburger, composed a successful hit from some of these elements – *North Circular Isolation (I'm only waiting)* – the most memorable verse from which went:

'Cos I'm feelin' blue
I go out sniffin' glue
If I wanna get some love
I gotta push and shove
'Cos all them sparklin' eyes
Is just for other guys
(Chorus: Woo! Woo! Other guys)

This brings us to a golden rule for love lyrics: these SHOULD NEVER BE HAPPY. Happy love songs went out with Doris Day and clean teeth. Modern love lyrics are all about desertion in a Motorway Cafe. All your groups are to be instructed to look thoroughly disgruntled as they perform their numbers, which is generally not very difficult for them when they realise what they are being paid. One of my friend Jarvis's more esoteric bands, Earwax, continually pick their noses and examine the findings during their two-hour act.

DRESS

The dress should match the sound. If the group is a revival they can dress in their old cast-offs; if they are *avant-garde* they can dress in luminous plastic with things sticking out of their ears. Anything goes: my group, The Black Tie, dresses only in paper bags, while Paper Bag dresses in black ties. The late Buddy Pickle wore a garment made of live scorpions. Distinctive dress has a useful spin-off for the gifted money-maker. One of my acquisitions, The Drool, has set a profitable trend in discoloured sweatshirts which should cover the cost of gold *lamé* upholstery on the spare Jag. All groups should avoid roll-neck sweaters as these are worn by All-Round Entertainers.

THE LANGUAGE OF SOUND

With sounds changing all the time a complicated system of names has grown up to describe all the different ways of producing permanent injury to the ear drums. This can be confusing to the entrepreneur just moving into the market, but it is important to know the *mot juste* to capture the right set of stars for your personal constellation. The following is a list of the more important terms in currency at the moment, which will help you converse sympathetically with your discoveries before getting your personal confidential assistant to whip out the Contract:

Two-tone Music produced on only two notes.

Riff Nasty infection of the scalp produced by too many nights under the spotlights.

Heavy metal Gold discs.

Lead guitar Musical instrument used to produce heavy metal.

28

Ska   Music produced on three or four notes.

Funk   Desire to run away from loud and ugly sound.

Punk   As funk, but human.

Country and Western   Music produced in the fields around Truro.

Disco   What slips, under the influence of reggae.

Soul   Still small voice that is supposed to be unbuyable; not worth bothering about.

Album   Collection of songs wrapped up in clever presentation pack carrying illustration nothing at all to do with music, especially pictures of bananas or dead goldfish.

Gig   Evening spent with Riff and Moog.

ALL-ROUND FAMILY SONGSTERS

Once your stars have had a few years of success they can start becoming a bit of a problem. They are too old to appeal to the Young, and still too disgusting to appeal to the Old. You have to work on a change of image to make them acceptable to a different market. Of course, if you are lucky they might get killed in an air crash, which means you can go on releasing posthumous records for the six or seven years without having to pay them anything. Some groups are best allowed to sink noisily back into obscurity. A few individual stars *can* make the transition into all-round family songsters, in which condition they are a pretty reliable cash commodity for years to come. They have to be weaned off all the old ways that gave them their rebellious charisma, like eating their instruments, or doing Interesting Things with microphones. Your newspaper releases must feature your female warblers in the company of young animals and Old Age Pensioners, preferably both together. Get the male ones into West End musicals, where they can display their *all-round talent*, and learn to speak words. Encourage appearances on television programmes where vicars and sociologists discuss the *mores* of the Young. Foster clean living and the regular use of dental floss.

> 'MONEY TALKS; BIG MONEY SHOUTS' R.M.

The kind of sound produced by your stars should change in harmony with their image. I particularly favour songs about bluebirds and loved ones temporarily parted, but most songs to do with the

Finer Side of human emotions will do, e.g. about sick, faithful dogs, or yearnings to be wed. Even if the words are sad, the music should be happy. Females should be taught how to belt out the tunes at the top of their voices while waving their arms about to signify deep emotion, and they will be judged particularly profound if they can sob and grin at the same time. Males should adopt a relaxed, intimate smile of the kind you would bestow upon a large cheque made out to your External Account. They may be permitted to include the odd ditty about how they have suffered at the hands of the opposite sex, but the wry smile will clearly indicate that these unfortunate events have happened to somebody else.

Women all-rounders should dress in shimmering creations deeply cleaved from the top and slashed up both thighs. Even when the various revealing incisions of my talented triller Ruby Deeply finally ran together during a strenuous top C, the resulting *brouhaha* in the media only served to further her reputation. Males, on the other hand, should be attired in more sober suits of tasteful *lamé*, which will not detract from the sincerity of the words gasped into the clutched microphone. You are aiming for *glamour*, not clamour. Glamour is the excitement of the unattainable, the allure and the mystery of the Stage, and the best way to get cash with *panache*.

You will be lucky to hang on to your vocalist long enough for him or her to become an Institution. This is the final stage of development of the *artiste*. Now they do not have to sing at all, but can stagger round clasping the microphone and mumbling the words of the songs that brought them fame, in a voice cracked with Deep Emotion and spirits aged fourteen years in the wood. Glamour alone is necessary, although a plastic surgeon helps.

REPRISE

● Music is a sound investment.

● Buy cheap and dirty; sell expensive and loud.

● Rebellion is the hard currency of Youth; *Schmalz* is the soft underbelly of Middle Age. There is a sound for each.

● He that pays the piper calls the tune; it should be *You* who finishes up with a fistful of notes every time.

● Bands may perish, but the backing must go on.

HOW
TO BECOME EXTREMELY
WELL HEELED
FROM COLLECTING THINGS

For most normal people a good collection of money seems to satisfy their acquisitive instincts. However, I have noticed that more and more denizens of the International Set are becoming *cognoscenti* and *aficionados* of the Ancient Object. 'A thing of beauty is a Joy for Ever' as the poet neatly put it (especially as it can be cashed in for money when collateral is getting a little on the dodgy side.) There is an added satisfaction in reclining on a Renaissance *chiffonier* after a hard day of selling short knowing that every day it gets older and it will realise that much more in Christie's or the King's Road. I usually leave the price tags on my *objets d'art* for this reason.

The guiding principle is: 'Old is Gold'. The older something is the more likely it is to contribute towards that custom-built Mazerati. (Old custom-built Mazeratis are particularly sought-after.) The only exception to this is when things get *very old indeed*, e.g. Roman, because then they are often all in bits. (From what I have seen in Museums and other Shrines of the Ancient, the Romans were pretty bad at looking after their pots and jewellery because they are nearly all broken. Greek sculptures are even worse.)

It used to be that something had to be at least 100 years old to be

31

called 'Antique' and if it was any older it was called 'Period', but fortunately this narrow-minded view has not prevailed, and nowadays it is worth investing in anything which hails from those more leisurely days when there were still traditional craftsmen working at skills which had changed little for hundreds of years. *I keep anything made before 1963.*

This opens up new worlds for those of us who can appreciate the aesthetic side of a healthy balance in the Deposit Account. And a fine collection of Ashanti nose rings is always the focal point for any of those cocktail parties you throw for Luminaries of the local Chamber of Commerce. I know from personal experience that more than one Big Name behind a chain of betting shops displays his artistic side in the privacy of his mansion surrounded with mature evergreen shrubs by buffing up his collection of Antique Medicinal Leeches or eighteenth-century tooth-extraction apparatus. My own collection of Toothpicks through the Ages gives me a unique insight into how our forebears winkled out those irritating bits of gristle from between their molars. Your collection enables you to get educated and rich at the same time.

Of course some of the high-quality stuff does run a bit expensive. So a **word of warning** here. If a chap in a blue blazer and cravat, driving a 1.8 litre Ford Cortina, offers you some original Hepplewhite ironing boards for £35 the chances are that the items in question are *not* 100 per cent bona fide. They may have been made by Fred Hepplewhite from Sutton Coldfield. My friend Jarvis had a very nice line in original Da Vincis which were done by Len Da Vinci of the Ball's Pond Road School, rather than Leonardo famed for his backward handwriting and enigmatic smile.

Some of these antique merchants use a lot of jargon to describe the Glories of the Past, which may seem a little confusing at first. Here is a list of some of the more important words which should help you to become a connoisseur without any difficulty:

Piece (as in, 'a fine piece this') – Expensive.

Quattrocento Italian artistic work costing more than £400.

Inlay The opposite of Outlay.

Marquetry Fiddly bit of furniture sold in markets.

Chaise Longue Settee with only one arm.

Commode Originally a chest of drawers, then designed to cover up sanitary apparatus. An *excritoire* is a French edition of the same thing.

Lacquer cabinet Where the seventeenth-century smart set kept their

VSOP and other liquor, often with fetching sylvan scenes on the doors.

Parquetry As marquetry, but on the floor.

Farquhartry Applied to the seventeenth-century ceramic work of Bonifacius Farquhar, which is now much sought after by collectors. His work was only rediscovered three years ago after centuries of neglect, and as a result there is not much about. Most of what there is has been acquired by: Farquhartry Market Cornering Co. Ltd, 45 Greater Dealgate, York.

Ming Dynasty Famous Chinese potter, who churned out a lot of stuff; so did his grandfather Tang.

Chinoiseries Things turned out in Chinese style – i.e. small, numerous and red.

Gilt What the owner feels when he drops his best Coalport.

Coalport A precious article on no account to be dropped.

Musket Old gun; a pair of crossed muskets is an obligatory embellishment to any escutcheon worth the name.

Escutcheon Place to hang muskets; escutcheons have been known to get blots on – these can usually be wiped off with a *What-not*.

Rococo More baroque than *Baroque*, less decadent than *Fin-de-siècle*, and also earlier than the latter.

Patination Very important this. We experts can tell exactly how old a fine Piece is by the nature of the Patination. This skill cannot be taught – it is learned through handling Fine and Rare examples of the Master Carpenter's Art in Great Houses, which I can usually manage once a week or so.

Pewter Metal used for tankards and mugs distinguished by its patination.

GETTING ANTIQUES CHEAP

There is no need to pay a King's Ransom for something Old and Aesthetically top-notch. A true devotee of the Money-Making Scheme will have to cut out the middleman to go directly to the source of the goodies, i.e. people's homes, wherein lurks an Aladdin's Cave of unsuspected treasures. Several of my neighbours in Mediterranean watering spots owe their leisurely afternoons on the patio to shrewd footslogging around the suburbs of Barnsley, while more than one celebrated exponent of the orchestrated versions of the Hits of Paul McCartney has his *salon* graced by a piece that originated in the villages surrounding Tiverton. The trade of the 'knocker' can be a lucrative one, and one that lifts the Thing of

Beauty from an *environs* where it may be wasted as a receptacle for empty Daddies Sauce bottles to one where it will be appreciated by someone of Good Taste and piles of the folding stuff. Of course, some people will be a little reluctant to part with their possessions, and the following technique is a tried and tested one in this situation:

● Get inside the door by saying you are doing a thesis on Domestic Motifs in the latter half of the twentieth century from the nearest University Sociology Department.

● Pretend to be bowled over by the flights of china swans over the mantlepiece or the *Souvenir of Margate* ashtray and similar absolute Rubbish. Meanwhile cast your eyes around for any of the Good Stuff.

● Offer a fiver for the flight of swans, or model of Princess Margaret made from sea shells, etc.

● 'Notice' the good item by accident. By a strange co-incidence your mother has a matching item that goes to make up the set. The poor lady is suffering from a rare and incurable condition of the kidneys and the said item may well bring back the twinkle into her old eyes, even though it is valueless in those of the World. Offer a quid.

● With any luck they will refuse your offer for the swans, but take the quid for *Meissen Kleinplastik.* Another priceless object will have been wrested from the philistines for the connoisseur, with all due pecuniary perks to the finder.

As so often with Creative Money-making, it is only a question of finding something that somebody does not want and selling it to somebody who wants it, even if the person that has it does not know what it is, and the person that wants it does not know where it came from. This is one of the Conundrums of Capitalism.

Once you have made a few decent killings you can start employing your own team of 'knockers'.

STAMPS

These small gummed squares or rectangles of paper are widely regarded as one of the best media for the high-speed acquisition of a Comfortable Lifestyle – and with good reason, because the 1856 British Guiana penny stamp is now worth half a million pounds, an appreciation rate of 20,000,000,000 per cent, which is not bad. People who bought these stamps back in 1856 and did not hang on to them must be kicking themselves now.

All you have to do with stamps is to stick them into *albums* and then wait and you will become hugely well-heeled. You must be careful not to bruise their patinations or blot their escutcheons, as this lowers their value. The only snag is you have to know which stamps to keep; for example, the 1857 St Lucia twopenny blue is still only worth twopence because it is hardly possible to buy a Giant Kilobag of Colonial Assorted without running into at least half a dozen of the little devils. So collect only rare ones.

Stamp collecting is now becoming very specialised, so many people with an eye for the Long-Term Investment collect only one kind of stamp, e.g. stamps from one country only, although this is difficult in the case of Monaco because they change their stamps twice a week because of all the stranded gamblers writing home for more money. For myself, I only collect stamps worth more than £400 which can be purchased for under a fiver, as I have found this is the most profitable kind of Collecting. Or you can collect First Day Covers which are on sale whenever you find immensely long queues at the Post Office. This Scientific Approach to stamps is known as Philately, after a Mr Philip Atterly, its earliest exponent, who now lives in Considerable Luxury in one of those Pacific Islands with mangoes in the middle of its 6 cents purple.

Stamps come in two varieties: *definitives* and *commemoratives*. Definitives are the ordinary little ones with the king's head on; Commemoratives are the big ones showing mangoes or elephant seals in the mating ritual. The true initiate does not bother with these *per se* – he only collects ones that have gone wrong for one reason or another. These *errors* are very interesting in showing small blobs on the Queen's neck at 500 times magnification. This makes them very valuable, particularly to people with powerful microscopes.

A few technical terms to help you compete with the professional:

Perforation (abbr. Perf.) Little holes between stamps to keep them apart. *Imperf.* stands for Imperfect Perforations, which are the kind that always result in dislocation of the Queen's neck.

Penny Black Girl who appears on the earliest British stamp.

Postmark Attempt to obliterate design of stamp by postman.

Postman Courier who brings stamps to the collector.

Watermark Valuable smudge on stamp when dropped by postman into a puddle.

Postage dues Special stamp that tells you that you have not put a stamp on a letter. These are cheap stamps to collect.

Charity Stamp For typical set of these send only £5 to General Post Office, Lesser Masteronia, Outer Antilles.

Money-making hints. These days philately has expanded to include all aspects of the postal system – covers, postmarks, stamp books, etc., etc. But a few postal accessories so far seem to have escaped the attention of the philatophiles; invest in these NOW and cash in on the future:

- **Collect** the sticky bits of paper from around sheets of stamps. Yards of the stuff is usually just *lying around* in the Post Office. Once you start collecting armfuls of this valuable investment you will find it hard to put down!

- **Collect postmen**. This rapidly dwindling resource is the investment of tomorrow. Postmen come in two main types: *definitives*, which are the ordinary little ones that get bitten by dogs and destroy correspondence by trying to push it through keyholes, and *commemoratives*, the large colourful ones that try to deliver the mail by breaking down the door. Take my word for it, automation will replace these collectibles within the next few years.

- **Collect pillar-boxes**. The old-fashioned 6-foot red will soon be discontinued so collect them *now* while there is still time. Special *albums* for mounting your collection available from: Masterphilia, 6 Publicity Drive, Birmingham 15.

The true visionary among collectors does not merely follow the dictates of Art and Rarity. For those with a dedication to Profit without Expenditure effortless fortunes are to be made from the humblest artefacts, freeing YOU to join famous writers of fiction for women's magazines on the slopes at St Moritz. Just remember, when the Romans threw their disused credit cards into the waste bin, THEY did not realise that one day these articles would be sought-after antiques now residing on velour plinths in the Jean-Paul Getty Museumerama.

There is no doubt that collecting can become a bug. But it *pays* to become an expert: 'Knowledge is Power', as Alaric the Goth expressed it. There is a lot to be said for acquiring a *very* specialised collection, like 10 per cent life-size models of the Empire State Building made from Ronson Lighters, because then nobody will know as much about the subject as you do. Once you have cornered the market you can start a Newsletter to bring all the other collectors in contact and to push up the prices. My own Metropolitan Litter Bins Newsletter (Motto: 'Waste Not, Want Not') paid for the addition of the Solarium in my Scilly Isles retreat.

To decide what to collect you should follow the simple set of rules – The Collector's Creed – that I have devised for your guidance:

- Collect things that normally get thrown away. Because such objects are usually jettisoned with a shrug it follows logically that

36

after a while *very few of them will remain*. They will then be sought after by people who wished they had not thrown them away when they had them. I *predict* that Kentucky Fried Chicken boxes will catch on. Collect them NOW before everybody does.

● Collect *unusual* things. There are some manufactured objects which are so unusual that very few are made, and even fewer sold. These are eminently collectable. I refer to models of Princess Margaret made out of painted sea shells, and sets of False Teeth made out of Southend rock, or covers for toilet rolls designed to look like pork pies. Most people will consign these to oblivion within hours of purchasing them – YOU alone will keep them until they are sought after as late twentieth-century *grotesqueries*.

● Collect breakable things. Many things nowadays are so poorly made that they break almost immediately. These are valuable investments, because pretty soon everybody that actually *uses* these objects busts them, and they join that vast shipment of valuable *ephemera* to the *municipal dump*. Anything Made in Taiwan belongs to this category, and most things Made in England, especially propelling pencils. The important thing to remember is *never use these objects more than once*: wrap them carefully in cotton wool (unless this is made in Taiwan) and place them securely in a wooden crate until the price rises.

● Collect *edible* things. This is the collectable for the twenty-first century. Encase the well-known delicacies of today in perspex blocks to protect them from Time's Corruption, and you will be the *only person* to recall the different manufacturing designs of the Mars Bar for the coming generations, or the history of the Humbug, on which I count myself an authority.

WHAT TO COLLECT NOW

People are catching on to collecting. This is not surprising when even something collected new a month ago is already worth more in the shops today. Here are just a few of the *objets de virtu* which are worth forking out a couple of fivers for, which will one day attract brisk bidding at Sothebys.

Records Old records are breaking new records, especially those made by the New Orleans Tub Thumpers in the 1830s. Go for the stuff everybody else passes by: Alma Cogan singing Ivor Novello's favourite fireside hits, or Reginald Dixon at the Wakefield Town Hall Hammond Organ, or Ivor Novello singing Reginald Dixon's greatest hits.

Art Deco Now is the time to collect lampshades made from intertwined 'flappers', and models of the Black Bottom and the Wall Street Crash.

Art Flimso 1964–5. Distinctive style combining simplicity and fragility, pioneered during these crucial years for the Arts. Few *working* examples of furniture of this period are now extant, and should be collected NOW.

War relics My friend Jarvis recommends that gas masks and grenades are worthwhile moneyspinners for tomorrow. Such *memento belli* can often be bought cheap off people with shell shock. See *Nazis for Profit* by J. Jarvis, Belsen Books (£5.95).

Pot lids Late nineteenth century. Often found by digging over Victorian rubbish dumps, which is where the Victorians went to throw their pot lids.

Books I recommend collecting *all* the editions of *Roderick Masters' Book of Money-Making Schemes*.

Mickeymousiana Now is the time to invest in all those things made in the likeness of Mickey Mouse, though only those with lots of storage room should embark on this particular collection. Soap, bottles, watches, books and other *bric-a-brac* will form a fascinating commentary on the Age of this most diminutive of Entrepreneurs. Rarest of all is the Mickey Mouse condom, which was soon withdrawn on grounds of bad taste by Minnie Mouse.

Money boxes A collection of money boxes will be a constant reminder of the Important Things in life, and can always be left lying around in case one of your visitors feels like finding out how they work. The traditional pig *motif* is only one of a thousand: I have examples in my collection modelled after twenties flappers, hand grenades, pot lids, books, Mickey Mouse and *excritoires*. This is the only Investment to keep your money in that you can keep your money in. The definitive work on this fascinating hobby is *Plus ça change* by R. Maitre, Faille d'on Press (887 guineas).

Book ends Useful collections of these, often designed as Mickey Mouse *rampant*, can be used to prop up your collections of *Roderick Masters' Book of Money-Making Schemes*.

White elephants A collection of these can be used to prop up your collection of book ends, which otherwise always fall over. See *Elephants for Collectors*, Pachyderm Press (£9.95).

Things from Christmas Crackers Readers will have noticed how all the contents of Christmas Crackers have entirely vanished by December 29th. A fortune can be made by carefully preserving these *ephemera* for posterity. Some of the Jokes in my collection are already valuable antiques.

Plastic fruit Plastic is the *papier mâché* of the second half of the twentieth century, and is a valuable long-term investment. I recommend specialising in fruit, which can be left in piles on the *chiffonier* for visitors to admire. Connoisseurs particularly seek the early Tesco *Green Pippin* for its charming artificiality, but the Woolworth *Grapes* of 1954 is now being acknowledged as one of the masterpieces of the *genre*. It is my belief that the *Split Pineapple with Ice Cubes* is the best bet for the 1990s, combining as it does an understated *insoucience* with a capacity for holding ice cubes.

Jokes Even now some of the rarer examples from the early days of the Practical Joke are commanding good prices, as a glance at the Collector's Journal *Invisible Ink* will reveal. The 1901 *split finger* is only exceeded in value by the prototype *Naughty Doggie*, while *Squeaking Camembert* is my own personal tip for the Big Climber over the next few years.

COLLECTING FOR THE FUTURE

There is somebody to collect almost anything, so you have to be exceptionally *au fait* with the aesthetic *ambience* of the 'found object' (*objet truffé*) to apply The Collector's Creed to the future. As with all Money Matters, Demand creates Value, Value creates a Market, the Market needs Supply, and the Supplier is the one with the large pile of notes and the best view at Cowes Week. Financial genius is recognising what will be in Demand before people know that they will be demanding it, and cornering most of the Supply. Most books only tell you what is *already* in demand, thereby stimulating demand, and pushing up the prices, so that the author of *The Cobblestone Collector's Compendium* can make even more of a killing. Here I will admit you to the secrets of what will be sought after by museums and connoisseurs in the year 2000, secrets previously available only to my most intimate circle, and the subscribers to *Roderick Masters' Money-making Monthly* (Collector's Corner by 'Magpie').*

First, I am certain that *paper cups* will acquire a big following in the years to come. Most of these are thrown away today, but remember that the same was true of Chelsea Ware hundreds of years ago, which is why there is so little of it about now. Some of the rare *software* cup varieties are almost unobtainable, probably because of wholesale destruction when it was discovered that the bottoms fell out. The same is true of the models with the paper handles pioneered by British Rail, known in the cup-collecting fraternity by the affectionate nickname of 'Wobbly'. The 'goblet' variety with holder is

* 'Magpie's' collected articles are available from:
    Magpie,
      The Rookery,
        Riffling-under-the-Jumble,
        Glos.

much in use now, but because these melt at anything warmer than tepid, I firmly believe that they will soon become a rarity.

Second, *computer errors* will become a *sine qua non* to all collectors of *errata*. Computer errors on bank statements in the customer's favour are especially rare items.

Third, *birth control devices* are very much a twentieth-century *genre*, and the majority of them are already discontinued rarities. Many of those that fit on the more Intimate Regions are designed in interesting shapes, and their materials have that Durability which is the characteristic of all Art. Some of the Interior Designs are even more interesting: little fishes, delicate springs, leafy shapes. There is every reason to suppose that these will become real rarities before the end of the century.

HOW
TO BECOME
GROSSLY RICH
FROM RELIGION

There is money in God.

Never before in the history of Human Endeavour have so many been looking for an Answer to all those ineluctable questions such as 'Why are we here?' 'What are we here for?' and 'Have we been here before?'. To become enormously rich from Religion all you need is a profound insight into the Human Condition, a deeply spiritual nature, a convinced belief in the sanctity of Man, and Genuine Desire to make money. I am religious myself: in poorer days scarcely a Sunday would pass without my dipping my hand into the collection plate.

To start a religion you need followers, or disciples as they were called in times long ago. This is not difficult. My friend Jarvis started a religion in San Francisco. All he did was hang a notice saying 'I am the light' around his neck, while holding a 60 watt light bulb aloft in his right hand. In three weeks he had 10,000 followers, or disciples to give them their proper name, and was living in a desirable ranch-style church in Beverley Hills.

41

Religion especially attracts those who find life a meaningless charade, who are lost in the Urban Nightmare. Many people turn to religion because of some private grief, such as the loss of a loved one, terminal cancer, or because they have given all their money to some other religious sect. They are fruit ripe for the plucking for anyone who like myself has a deeply spiritual nature.

All religions need a name. Here are some acceptable names for religions:

The Seminary for the Divine Light

The Children of Ecological Transfiguration

The Church of United Faith and Freedom

The House of Mandragore

The Church of Transcendental Pleasure Inc.

The Yonic School of Beatitudes

The Legion of Love and Life

Here are some unacceptable names for religions:

The Penge and Norwood Missionary Association

The Christians

W. C. Bindweed's 'Life is for Living' Brigade

The Failed Persons' Spiritual Uplift Society

The Mary Whitehouse Fun Sunday Club

Once you have a name and some disciples the next thing is to cast the net to secure all the Lost Souls who are thirsting after spiritual uplift and enlightenment. As a model, take the following document mailed to thousands of prospective converts.

THIS DOCUMENT CONTAINS
INFORMATION VITAL TO THE WELFARE
OF YOU AND YOUR FAMILY

What do you want to happen to **YOU**?

A. Sit for ever on clouds eating your favourite goodies, surrounded by glamorous and famous people
☐ tick if yes

B. Be roasted over eternal fires while being prodded by horrible ugly creatures with pitchforks
☐ tick if yes

What do you want out of **LIFE**?

A. Be happy and loved and respected by everyone
☐ tick if yes

B. Feel lousy most of the time and very unpopular
☐ tick if yes

What do you want out of **LOVE**?

A. Be enormously attractive to the opposite sex, even into old age
☐ tick if yes

B. Never make it with anyone, not even your **DOG**
☐ tick if yes

What do you want out of **HEALTH**?

A. Feel always on top of the world, and die peacefully of old age
☐ tick of yes

B. Suffer a variety of rare and crippling diseases with no known cure
☐ tick if yes

What do you want from **FORTUNE**?

A. Be famous and have lots of ready cash
☐ tick if yes

B. Be broke and of no fixed abode
☐ tick if yes

When you pass on, what do you want people to think?

A. There goes one helluva great guy/gal
☐ tick if yes

B. Never heard of him/her
☐ tick if yes

If you have answered by ticking *any* of questions A above, then you should take advantage of the **FREE OFFER** to join **THE CHURCH** of **ENLIGHTENMENT AND SPIRITUAL HARMONY** (C.A.S.H.). Find the secret of life! **DISCOVER FOR YOURSELF THE MYSTERIES** of success and inner harmony.

Like Mrs A. Filbert of 45 Playtex Gardens, Peebles, who writes

'Before I discovered **THE CHURCH OF ENLIGHTENMENT AND SPIRITUAL HARMONY** my life was a succession of nervous breakdowns and financial disasters. Now, thanks entirely to you, I have a T registration Ford Cortina, and have been asked to become the next Chairwoman of Ancilliary activities at the Women's Institute . . .'.

YES, you, too, can discover the **INNER SUCCESS** you have always craved. **IT IS ONLY A QUESTION OF TRUSTING YOURSELF TO A HIGHER SOURCE OF POWER, WHICH OUR UNIQUE METHOD OF BIOTRONICS* CAN GIVE YOU.** Tune into a higher plane of consciousness, and see the cash come rolling in!

DON'T DELAY! FILL IN THE FORM TODAY

I am interested in joining **THE CHURCH OF ENLIGHTENMENT AND SPIRITUAL HARMONY** (C.A.S.H.) ☐ yes

I wish to take advantage (no obligation) of the **FREE OFFER**
☐ yes

THEN SEND YOUR CHEQUE FOR £20 NOW to:
Master of eternal tranquillity (external account)
   Box 567,
     Enlightenment Villas,
     Sutton Coldfield.

N.B. **VERY IMPORTANT** ... Mark all your payments 'PAY C.A.S.H.'

* Patents pending

With this kind of publicity it will only be a very short time before you become hugely wealthy. Of course, it helps to have some idea of Religion in order to provide the deep personal self-knowledge and sense of Inner Fulfilment that your many converts crave. Fortunately my own depths of perception into the Ultimate Meaning of Life are so profound that I may save the tiro making his first essay into this field a good deal of effort by enumerating the Principal Routes to Perfection.

I have no doubt that in my previous incarnation I was privy to all the Esoteric Secrets which have been lost to our present civilisation, which is obsessed by the Material and the Transient at the expense of the Deeper Values which those of us who are naturally spiritual, like myself, so rightly despise. However, as Calvin Coolidge said 'Idealism that is not tempered by pragmatism is like betting on a Good Horse that is running the Wrong Race.'

THE PRINCIPAL ROUTES TO PERFECTION
© Money-making Schemes (Bahamas), Inc.

1 REINCARNATION OF GOD

YOU are the recipient of the IMMORTAL WISDOM via THE GREAT CHAIN OF BEING stretching from the great Prophets of Old by way of King Arthur and Nostradamus, famed for predicting Hitler, the Atomic Bomb and the Sex Pistols. All you require of your followers is UNCONDITIONAL WORSHIP, giving up all their worldly goods in the pursuit of the calm that passes all understanding. For this it is necessary to have a Top Notch Accountant as your No. 2, so that you may devote yourself to your burgeoning Flock. Much of your spiritual business will be conducted in a Stately Home surrounded by extensive grounds, lime trees and electric fences. These last may be necessary to keep out relatives who mistake your concern for religious guidance with crass materialistic pursuits: these have to be dealt with by demonstrating your magisterial presence, infused through the generation of the Prophets. If that fails it helps to have some big men as acolytes.

For guidance of those who have given their All to follow you it is advisable to issue them with regular Bulletins containing the distillation of the Wisdom which your direct route to the Most High has vouchsafed. Here are some useful examples. They should be handed out each day on roneo'd sheets issued from the Tabernacle in which you reside.

- 'We are all cracked vessels; the **WISE ONE** is the glue of Life.'

- 'To give your ALL is to gain your Freedom.'

- The **WISE ONE** saith, 'The sound of one hand clapping is the heartbeat of Enlightenment.'

- 'Blessed is he that hath Nothing, for he has Everything, whereas he that hath Something hath Nothing, for the **WISE ONE** saith that everything which is a Thing, that also is nothing, whereas those things that are given away become Everything.'

- 'The road to the Palace of Wisdom is through the Door of Humility, and make sure you wipe your feet on the Doormat of Confession, lest you bring in the Mud of the World.'

You, of course, are the **WISE ONE**.

If your name is Bert Gummidge, or Ted Rowbotham, or Hugh Rundle, it is a good idea to change your name if you intend to become a Wise One. My own experience suggests that names like THE GREAT THOTH, PHILARDROBIUS OF TARA or THE MASTER OF CLARITY serve very well for most purposes. There is plenty of scope for imagination here.

Important. If you wish to be a Supreme Master of the Mystic Secrets of the Ages it is important that you never appear dressed in suit and tie. A simple, white dress trimmed with ermine will suffice, and it is a good idea to wear a necklace of dangling rhinoceros teeth or mandrake roots just in case.*

2 BORN AGAIN CHRISTIAN

You are the direct inheritor of the mantle of the great EVANGELISTS: St Paul and St John. You have been chosen to spread the Word, to reclaim the damned from their sojourn with the Devil, and to divert the wealth which might otherwise be squandered on Food and Clothes into that Higher Food for which the World has no price.

To achieve this all you have to do is keep going on about how

---

* A wide selection of such accessories is obtainable from:
Metaphysical Accoutrements (Barnsley) Ltd,
   c/o Masters Enterprises,
     Featherstonehaugh Terrace,
      Wick.

sinful everybody is and how the only salvation is the Lord and how you are the humble mouthpiece of the Lord and how the Lord's work needs funds and how the Man in the dark blue suit at the back will help you to your contribution. There's nothing like making people feel bad to make them feel good.

You can also try 'laying on of hands' which consists of you placing your hand on top of somebody's head and then taking it off again. You can also dip all your converts into a large body of water and then let them dry off, which is called baptism.

If you have a tendency towards being an intellectual, as I do myself, then it may be profitable to have a good knowledge of the Bible which is a well-known source for quotations of a Spiritual and Appropriate Nature. If you have a bad memory for lines then you should invoke the Book of Cashin,* which is a little-known scroll somebody dug up from the Dead Sea which contains many quotations particularly spiritual for The Modern Age and especially for large corporate organisations e.g.

- 'He that investeth a goodly part of his worldly goods with the Lord's appointed shall reap an hundredfold, all things being equal', Cashin IV, v. 5.

- 'And the Lord spake unto Cashin in Dorag Gath, *which being translated is* the Street called Wall, saying: gather ye the men bearing large pieces of gold, for they are chosen of the Lord to wax extremely Rich', Cashin VI, v. 9.

- 'And lo there is rot in the vine, and in the Treasury also the weevil grows fat, and *I say unto you* that only in the Legions of the Lord will all that thou holdest dear be safe from the locust', Cashin XXI, v. 93.

If you happened to have been christened with a name like The Great Thoth, or Philardrobius of Tara, it is a good suggestion to change your name to something more acceptable for an Evangelist, like RICK FORTHRIGHT or STEVEN GOODSIR, but most names that do not belong to an ethnic minority will do.

Important notice. If you are to be an Immaculate Mouthpiece for a Higher Being it is important that you wear a suit and tie at all times. You must also be very *sincere*, always gazing everybody straight in the eyes, which I know many people find difficult. I have found it

* Copies available from:
  M.M.S. Theological Publications,
  Featherstonehaugh Terrace,
  Wick
  (£10.99 p. & p. included).

is useful in producing a look of the deepest sincerity and concentration to imagine whoever was being addressed as a £20 note. Consequently I can summon up a look of sincerity every time.

3 SCIENTIFIC SALVATION

YOU have discovered a unique *scientific* method of helping those oppressed with self-doubt, *angst*, and alienation towards inner harmony and peace with the world. Your evident qualities for this role are your own inner harmony and sense of self-fulfilment, which you display to advantage on your private yacht.

You charge £1,000 for Moderate Happiness, £2,000 for Considerable Happiness and £3,000 for Absolute Happiness. This is easy to provide. Your highly trained staff spend all day hurling insults like 'fat slob' and 'insignificant worm' at the initiates, which helps them a good deal along the road to self-awareness. Those who are after Considerable Happiness are allowed to be rude to the people who have just joined, while those who have purchased Absolute Happiness can watch the whole proceedings from behind one-way mirrors.

At regular intervals you monitor progress with the help of the Black Box.* This is a sophisticated scientific instrument with many computers and dials. When the initiate is plugged in, the largest dial measures his progress on a scale from 1 to 3,000. Those who have expected Moderate Happiness get 1,000 at the end of the treatment, those who anticipate Considerable Happiness get 2,000, and those who have paid for Absolute Happiness get 3,000. They are usually very pleased to get the score they wanted and this makes them happy and feel that the scientific method has wrought its wonders.

Occasionally you get somebody who is not satisfied with the treatment, but they are usually Born-Again Christians.

---

* A selection of highest quality Black Boxes obtainable from:
Masters Technology Ltd,
Featherstonehaugh Terrace,
Wick.
(Send £20 for no obligation catalogue).

HOW TO GET
VERY RICH
FROM DEATH

Death is important. It is the quickest way money passes from one generation to the next. It is the last Big Deal in the Ledger of Life.

When people sense the approach of the Great Reaper they usually make a *will*. The will is an instruction manual containing details of who is going to get what. When beneficiaries are 'mentioned' in a will it usually means that they get fifty quid and an ormolu clock. But somebody always gets the lion's share of any will, and this person should be YOU. Inheritance has the great advantage that it is the simplest way to become exceptionally affluent. I have inherited several large fortunes without even stirring from my *chaise longue* commanding a view of the golf course.

The simplest way to inherit a fortune is to be next of kin of the moribund person with the loot. Even this is not without its *hazards*:

● Your dying relative may wish to found a *charity* to help those less well-heeled than he was, like Italians. This should be prevented at all costs. Send him pamphlets through the post on the deviations practised by Italians.

● Another dreadful possibility is that he might decide to leave his wealth to the *poor and needy* branch of the family, often a vicar in Pontefract with eleven children. This eventuality can usually be averted by sending a telegram to the vicar to say that the company of the eleven children is urgently required at the bedside of the dying man. This often results in a quick death before the will can be changed.

● A third hazard and in many ways the worst is that the fading relative may develop a senile passion for cats' homes. This can become an *idée fixe* which is very hard to shift, although it is usually worth trying to introduce a couple of incontinent alley cats into the household. If this fails, *found a cat's home*. You are then the natural person to *administer* the feline fortune. I have several attractive residences dotted about the world, like *Château Chat* or *Tortoiseshell Towers*, in each of which I have occasionally caught a glimpse of a cat.

The worst thing that can happen to you is to be cut off without a penny. This usually happens when you have been caught doing something thoroughly untoward. Never kick cats in the home of a dying relative. The inheritance is the biggest boon to instant affluence since the Egyptians invented pyramid selling, and should be guarded with all the devotion you would normally reserve for a deal involving fragile commodities. To be the next of kin of a wealthy relative is a piece of luck that seldom happens more than once in a lifetime: cherish it carefully.

THE RICH SHALL INHERIT

More often than not you are only one of a number of possible beneficiaries to share up the proceeds of Death; you may even be low on a list preceded by such persons as sons and daughters who feel they have some sort of right over the goodies to come. You should never feel daunted by such strong competitors. Remember: where there is a Will there is a way. As a rule such close relatives are not motivated by the love of money which makes you the natural guardian of inherited wealth. If your deals have been going particularly well you may already be familiar with the comforting propinquity of a well-stuffed wallet, but *do not let this interfere with your purpose*. How much better that the bulk of the assets should be directed towards one who knows how to look after healthy cash surpluses, than be squandered on school fees or dental treatment by improvident close relatives.

It is one of the Conundrums of Capitalism that your favourable financial state is a positive *advantage* in the inheritance stakes. This is because the rich person expiring from a nasty dose of cancer or Bright's disease finds nothing more depressing than to be surrounded on all sides by moist-eyed, impoverished relatives in ill-fitting suits. When they whisper that they have invested a large part of the family's life savings to make the journey from Pontefract he usually feels an overwhelming urge to disinherit them on the spot. He is obliged to be kissed by stammering and fleshless offspring, whose breath smells of cheap gum drops, an odour to which the Sick are peculiarly sensitive. For this reason you should encourage such visits from your more unprepossessing rivals, even to the extent of purchasing their offspring several pounds of Aunty Kitty's Raspberry Comfits.

> 'GREED IS WANTING MORE THAN YOU CAN POSSIBLY HAVE; SUCCESS IS GETTING IT' R.M.

The dying wealthy man wishes to remember quite different things from his numerous relatives in poor circumstances. He likes to be reminded of his greatest *coups*, of deals gone by, of rivals bankrupted and gone to the Great Reckoner before him. You should swot up on these. As Death beckons to him from the balcony of his elegant, Holland Park establishment he cannot but reflect on the nature of Mortality, the brevity of human existence, and how much VAT he has paid over the last few years. He realises that he *Can't Take It With Him*, and has a vision of the chipped fingernails of his deserving relatives sifting through the pile of gold that has survived him. This is the point at which you move in with the Indian ink and the brand-new Will form.

At exactly the same juncture your benefactor realises that if he leaves his fortune to YOU his money will live on, even though his mortal frame withers into dust. Under your *aegis* the cash will divide and multiply like so many great-grandchildren, and without making a mess on the carpet. He will sign in your favour. He will realise that the fortune should not be divided: a masterpiece like Michaelangelo's *Athlete holding a large flat coin* is no longer a masterpiece if it is bashed up into a number of subequal bits. Each of the other beneficiaries should be endowed with fifty quid and an ormolu clock.

Thanks to your wise counsel, the dying man will go to his grave happy in the thought that he clinched his last and best deal just before popping off. You will have brought calm where before there was agitation; after the Departure you will have earned yourself a decent recuperation period in Rallentando della Mare. Always have a couple of honest citizens hanging around to be witnesses to the Will, and burn all the old wills that may be stuck behind bookcases or stuffed in the *What-Not*.

A few **helpful hints** will help towards the happy *coup de grâce*:

- Never mention Death. This is always a depressing subject to somebody in a terminal state of lung cancer. Confine conversation to cheery comments about Tobacco Futures.

- Allow the occasional roll of pristine tenners to fall from your breast pocket on to the counterpane: the sight of large sums of cash builds up confidence.

- Let the sick man in on one of your deals; pay him back five-fold in cash the first time the subject of Wills comes up.

- Mention in passing various unpleasant and infectious rashes from which the other beneficiaries habitually suffer.

But I should give you *a* **word of warning** here. It is a mistake to anticipate the good news of your inheritance. The dying have a remarkable capacity for hanging on beyond their appointment with the Ultimate Cashier. My friend Jarvis botched the chance of a succulent inheritance by turning up at his Uncle Seth's with two removal vans, a dozen bottles of Veuve Cliquot, and wearing shoes which were obviously designed for dancing on graves. The old man had rallied in the night, and was looking better than he had for several months, in fact, ever since his 4-year-old great nephew had dropped a wet, boiled sweet on his electric blanket. He was well able to raise himself to the task of disinheritance, even though he shortly afterwards expired with the effort. For this reason I would strongly advise a long trip to check your Cayman Island brass plaques once the necessary alterations to the Will have been made in your favour. Your personal confidential assistant can make regular calls with bunches of grapes, and her dramatic *décolletage* may even assist a speedy *dénouement*.

> 'A FIVER IN THE HAND IS WORTH TWO FIVERS AT 15% COMPOUND
> INTEREST OVER SIX YEARS IN THE BUSH' R.M.

AUNTS

Statistics tell us that women live longer than men, which is why it is difficult to arrange a confidential appointment in Hyde Park without being accosted by half a dozen healthy dowagers. The reason for this comparative longevity probably resides in the fact that women are also statistically smaller than men, which means that there is not so much of them to wear out. Whatever the reason, the sad fact remains that your rich male acquaintance or relative often dies first, leaving the bulk of an indecently large fortune to his spouse of fifty years. Negotiations with such aunts can be much more tricky than with the male equivalent. Women are not normally so susceptible to the Higher Human Emotions, such as the desire to turn a huge profit with the minimum of outlay. They are not likely to be impressed by your tales of derring-do in the cut-and-thrust world of high finance, nor will they thrill to the finer details of the Birmingham Banana Bonanza. They are often deeply attached to the poorer members of the family, especially clergymen from Pontefract, and appear to be immune to the glutinous infections carried about by small children. They are a problem.

However, no problem is insuperable to those dedicated to the acquisition of what is rightfully theirs. Even ancient aunts have their Achilles' heels, located somewhere near their bunions. Your job is to seek out these weaknesses, become an indispensable *confidant* to the declining lady, and gently oust your younger competitors with tales of their cruelty to poodles. There is no single formula for success, and the prosecution of this task is one of the greatest tests of the dedicated money-maker. On the positive side, very few of the necessary sacrifices require much capital outlay, which means that deathbed attendance can be a particularly profitable way of spending the time when the coffers are a bit depleted. Here are a few of the Routes to the Loot:

- **Kissing**. Very necessary this. You must perform the ritual on greeting and departure; it must have just the right amount of warmth without ever spilling over into passion, which is decidedly *de trop*. It is worth practising the embrace with a consenting friend in the privacy of your own home. Cheeks and forehead only.

- **Jobs**. I have repeatedly observed that aged, ailing ladies are unable to perform domestic tasks like changing plugs or light bulbs. To undertake such mundane, if unpleasant operations has a most beneficial effect on your chances of inheritance. I attribute my large legacy from Mrs Mountjoy Farquhartington almost entirely to an afternoon spent unblocking her faucets.

- **Flowers**. The old and infirm of the female sex have an inexplicable attachment to these. It may be because of the sweetish smell they tend to exude, which is not unlike that of confidential personal assistants. A couple of bunches of the more expensive varieties always seem very acceptable, and can be delivered in your absence if you suddenly have to take off for Rio de Janiero to clinch a deal.

● **Gifts**. The most effective gift is a silver-framed photograph or artist's rendition of the dead spouse. This arouses sentimental reflections, and identifies YOU in the mind's eye with the departed one, often resulting in a couple of favourable codicils.

● **Never mention Age or Death**. Should the conversation take a morbid turn, deflect it with the gift of an individually wrapped, kirsch-filled chocolate made by Cholesterold's of Piccadilly.

CARE FOR THE OLD AND INFIRM

The approach of the Closing Balance brings with it inevitable changes. The brain becomes less able to handle the complicated details of financial transactions, and the Numbered Account of the memory becomes more like an open deposit box. The ship of the body changes to a frail barque, liable to take on water or split the rigging at any time. Certain organs even jump ship altogether, often resulting in unpleasant spillages on deck. These facts of biology present genuinely lucrative opportunities for those with a caring disposition as well as strong pecuniary motivation. For it often happens that decaying persons are without a home port of their own, a haven where they may lie at rest until they are ready for the breaker's yard. YOU can provide such a haven. And when Death finally comes you will receive your due reward, i.e. all the money, to allow you to further the work for future frail barques.

Many of those in your care will have had a life of privilege and pampering; they will expect the same to continue now. You should have a smart address for your Twilight Home, and the façade should be painted regularly to encourage the more conscientious relatives to entrust their difficult charges to your ministrations. The rents for such establishments can be a bit on the high side, but you can usually economise in other directions. The food costs are normally low, for example, because many old persons cannot remember when they had their last meal. Your highly trained staff are used to coping firmly with cantankerous types, and are very good at administering sedatives. High wages and good working conditions often encourage defectors from the prison service. And it is important to have a fully qualified doctor, who graduated from the Free University of Bangalore *summa cum laudanum*, who is able to put an appropriately florid signature on Death Certificates. Your team will ensure that the last days of your guests are spent as peacefully and as quickly as possible. It is surely a tribute to the quality of care at my own Eventide Estate '*Past Masters*' that not a word of criticism about it has ever reached the outside world. As a precaution, always double lock the front (and only) entrance.

'NEVER POUR GOOD MONEY AFTER BAD; ALWAYS OPEN A NEW ACCOUNT' R.M.

Gratitude, or *Grates Morphiae* to give it its medical name, often overwhelms your patients during their terminal days. They are over-come with a need to leave you a fat legacy to help you care for others in the same way. Receive such bequests in the proper spirit (quickly). At this juncture, it is not unusual for importuning relatives to wish to see your charges, but this should be resisted on clinical grounds, for such visits tend to disrupt the peaceful, spiritual equilibrium which months of your careful attention has brought about. There may be questions *post mortem* about the state of mind of the de-ceased, but your doctor will be able to confirm that the last days were probably the most tranquil that the deceased had ever known. The grave is impervious to accusations, and anyway you have special terms at the local crematorium.

A financial footnote here. It is not unknown for Cupid to wander into one of your twilight homes. Old ladies in particular are liable to experience a late flutter in the heart, touched perhaps by small gifts of food and other kindnesses. After many decades of Teabags for One they feel a need to leave the world in a state of togetherness. A chance to bring happiness, no matter how short-lived, should never be overlooked. Especially high-speed marriage services are arranged through the Visiting Chaplain of the CBCI (Church of Bodies Cor-porate and Incorporeal) and the Reverend Nosferatu does a special combined nuptial and last rites every other Sunday.

SUMMARY: DEATH IN A WORD

● Death, like 'money', is a five-letter word. While it is happening to somebody else it is your ally.

● You are a better person to look after a fortune than somebody who is dead.

● Dust to dust and cash to cash: the body withers and fades but the harder currency lingers on.

● Without death there would be no inheritance: you cannot cheat Death, but you *can* get it on your side.

● If you are having a somewhat lean time, Death can sometimes be your Last Trump.

HOW
YOU CAN MAKE
BIG MONEY
FROM SMALL ADVERTISEMENTS

Direct selling cuts out the Middleman and cuts you in for a bigger share of the profits. The fact that you are normally the Middleman shows you exactly how much profit you are cutting out. Many of those who now take their ease in architect-designed Spanish villas made their pile from selling implements for chopping aubergines into cubes as advertised in the columns of *Barter and Bargain*. The fact is: nobody can resist a bargain even when it is more than usually expensive. YOU acquire the goods, place an appropriate advertisement in an appropriate organ, and sit back to collect the postal orders. This is one of the easier ways to join the *entourage* of the famous. Sometimes it pays Big Dividends to Think Small.

There are some important RULES for words in small advertisements, which I am able to list for you as the result of many years of entrepreneurial enterprise.

● Always put the price in **BIG, BOLD** type.

Not £9.95, but **£9.95.**

● Always precede the price by the word '**ONLY**',

as in **ONLY £9.95.**

This is especially important if the usual price is £9.97.

● Always put some special feature inside a ragged star, symbolic of

unexpected detonation, e.g. **ONLY £9.95**

● Always have a small cartoon to depict the virtues of the object on offer. It is not a good idea to have a large picture of the object itself, as it may look disappointing in relation to the price. I favour a schematic lady of pleasing appearance, who is portrayed in a state of ecstasy. The vaguely drawn thing she is holding is the aubergine dicer on offer.

● It is always impressive to have a lot of very technical detail in extremely small type. Example: Exclusive Masterite was for years a closely guarded secret known only to a specially trained team of scientists at NASA (National Aubergine Slicing Assn). A unique combination of molybdenum, titanium, tungsten and steel, the last-named alone is employed in the technically astounding blade of this unique tool. Now it is available to a wider public for the first time. No more chopping aubergines with ordinary kitchen knives! Also clears drains and lags pipes. Send only. . . .

● Always add the words, 'With full, money-back guarantee if not satisfied' to the bottom of the advertisement. This means you can give a cheque time to clear before dispatching the goods, and if it bounces you guarantee to send it back, with a note expressing your dissatisfaction.

● The words, '**Direct from our Factory**!' inspire confidence that the object is a bargain.

● Free offers, or more correctly **FREE OFFERS** are always an added attraction. The offer is a brochure containing a long list of additional ways for the client to spend money.

PLACING YOUR ADS

We are in the Age of the Specialist Publication. Nowadays, there are special magazines for those who breed very large goldfish, and others for people who like to meet ladies dressed only in green perspex. For every Outlet there is an Organ. So if your goods are of a highly specialised nature you should place your advertisement in the appropriate journal. I prefer the greater challenge of going for the Nationals – like *Exchange and Mart* – where you are competing in the cut-and-thrust of open competition with those who have been doing small ads for generations. There are a number of categories that have consistently yielded high dividends to the entrepreneur, which I have listed for your guidance.

Vegetation can be divided into two varieties: *plants*, which are feeble, green things occasionally glimpsed under a thick mat of a second variety known as *weeds*. Gardeners have an insatiable appetite for new kinds of plants. Advertisements which read, 'Astonish your friends with the amazing Brazilian Goldfish-eating geranium!' are guaranteed to attract a flood of buyers.

When the plants refuse to eat goldfish, you send a repro. letter explaining that they only eat the Brazilian species. My friend Jarvis scored a notable *coup de cash* with the advertisement for 'the astounding Patagonian Century Plant . . . only £1.50, p&p'. The accompanying letter explained that the most astounding thing about the enclosed seed was that it has to be buried for a hundred years before it will germinate. The dedicated money-maker has plenty of scope for imagination here – remember, *a dead plant tells no lies*.

Fruit is also lucrative. Mr J.D. (pensioner) of Grimsby is a useful scheme in this case. He writes unsolicited letters to say that 'My friends were astonished at the 56 pounds of strawberries produced from your **NEW MIRACLE GIGANTO HYBRIDS . . .**'*. Mr J.D.'s friends are in an almost continuous state of astonishment, because of his extraordinary success in growing walnuts in window-boxes, or producing a rich mulch from old copies of the *Sporting Times*.

Exotic lingerie is a good illustration of the principle that *the less you sell the more you make*. Nylon can be turned into gold. Very little

* Testimonials made-to-measure from:
    Mr J.D. (pensioner) Ltd,
      Masters Lodge,
        Begonia Crescent,
          Grimsby.

material is used in the manufacture of these goods. Because the necklines plunge so low and the posteriors rise so high, they are very cheap to make. You can employ your staff in cutting out the bits between the legs of Marks and Spencer's knickers, which you sell as 'Mlle Babette, direct from the Place Pigalle'. Or you can sell the same number in black, wet-look leatherene under the name 'Fraulein Himmler'. Advertise with cartoons of 18-year-old ladies with their hands hidden in their hair (artists charge a lot for detailed drawings of fingers).

Lucky charms do especially well in mags connected with the Supernatural, like *Prognosis* and *The Medium is the Message*. Mr J.D. (pensioner) of Grimsby writes, 'My life was DOGGED by ILL LUCK. Honestly, I was the kind of bloke who couldn't walk under a ladder without getting a pot of paint on my trilby and dog doings on my Hush Puppies. Now all this has changed. Ever since I bought *The Pentacle of Mastrogora* (only £1.98 inc. VAT) even the 'doggies' have been coming in at No. 1. I felt I just had to write to say a personal 'Thank you' for the Charm that changed my FORTUNE. . . .' 'YES' you add, 'IT'S TRUE!!' 'Thousands whose lives have been ruined by one piece of bad luck after another, like Mr J.D. (pensioner) of Grimsby, have found their fortunes TRANSFORMED the moment they put the Pentacle around their necks. The secret of The Bilharzia of Mastrogora, guarded by fanatical priests for hundreds of years, can be yours by return if you send . . .', etc. You can knock up the pentacles in your workshop with a bit of resin and some jelly moulds. Include a printed leaflet explaining how to hang it around the neck. Illustration shows the object giving off mystic rays.

Audiovisuals. Electronics and similar scientific stuff is a growth industry and I recommend getting in on the ground floor before the balloon really goes up. I have had great success with my Swedish Adult Video Half (yes! Half!) Price Offer: 25-minute film features Swedish adults sitting around talking about Kierkegaard. This fulfils the terms of the Trades Descriptions Act.

Holidays. The glorious, freebooting days of Bargain Packages are now over, when clients were given the chance to *really* appreciate the open-air life in roofless hotels at Estartit. A new market has opened up in *Adventure Holidays*. These are a very good way to make money because they require very little organisation. Master Mariner (Adventure) Ltd offers a passport to the glamour and mystery of the Far East – 'The adventure of a lifetime'. The package consists of a one-way ticket to a small island off The Celebes, and the Adventure is trying to get back home again.

Self Help. This is very popular these days as more and more people Do It Themselves rather than Get Others In To Do It, because it is cheaper, at least until they have to Get In Somebody Else To Put It Right. There are a number of respectable, if modest, Money-Making Schemes from small advertisements showing how it can be done cheaper yourself. My own favourite is 'Build Your Own House for only £3.96 p&p (inc. VAT)'. For their money they get a plan of a very simple house, and a bundle of other leaflets including, 'Concrete mixers – are our prices MAD?, 'Erection Aids at Knock Down Prices', and 'Master Builder® Gas Central Heating Kits Bring Prices Down With A **BANG**!' Big money is to be made from the emergency Plumbing and Bricklaying Services listed on a separate sheet at the end.

Medical. A lot of people seem to be suffering from Migraine, Allergy, Constipation and general Asphyxia, which do not respond to conventional medicinal treatment or a week in Harrogate. They are the market for special medical Aids: Ginseng or Vitamin E can be a ray of hope for such dyspeptic unfortunates.

HIGHER CLASS IS A BIGGER DEAL

Most of the Schemes I have outlined so far are for advertising in journals with the kind of soft, absorbent paper used for wrapping fish and chips, or taken for Emergency Use on long walking tours. The higher end of the market comes on glossy material, in journals stuffed with advertisements extolling the expensive features of cheap cars, or the cheap price of expensive ones. Articles dotted between the ads are about hunger in an obscure part of Africa, or a tribute to some ageing journalist written by another journalist (who one day hopes for a tribute of his own). People often scan the advertisements in minute detail to distract themselves from the articles. The Golden Rule here is to ignore the Golden Rules I set out at the start of this chapter.

> 'A MAN IS JUDGED BY THE COMPANY HE TAKES OVER' R.M.

What you are selling here is *class*. Class is what things that lack
class have not got. (Class is signified by pretty ladies with an attack
of the sulks looking out over misty green fields. They are sulking
because they do not have even more class.) Class is expensive, and
it does not apologise for its expense, but makes a virtue of it. Class
is the way the Rich demonstrate they can buy the Things That Money
Cannot Buy. It is the great ally of the Schemer with a real sense of
pecuniary purpose, because it is the only Imponderable that adds to
the price without adding to the cost. Remember, class cannot be
bought, it can only *not* be bought by others who cannot afford it.

Never suggest that classy goods are a bargain: if they are a bargain,
they do not have class. The word to use is 'exclusive'. This word
comes from the latin *excludare*, meaning 'to shut out the riff-raff'.
People who buy classy goods want to believe that the only *other*
people buying the same commodities are even richer than they are.
The people at the top end buy things there are only one of, like
Picasso's *Still Life with Le Journal*. Often you do not have to mention
the price at all, and NEVER **feature** it, but you can tuck it tastefully
away in the bottom left of the advertisement in very small type.
Classy items are 'distinguished', 'intriguing' and 'produced by generations of fine craftsmen'. NEVER instruct the potential buyer to
'hurry while stocks last, everything must go in grand clearance!!', as
you would in the cheapo market. Classy goods are not even 'sold' in
the usual sense: they just pass gently into other hands.

There is no end to the things you can sell by small advertisements
in the class market:

● **Books** go down particularly well. These are bound in calf's hide
aged for 50 years in small cattle sheds on the banks of the
Garonne, and the title is hand-tooled in gold leaf. The contents do
not matter very much, although such numbers as Treatises on
Pederasty by little-known nineteenth-century aristocrats seem to
shift quickly with the old Etonian market.

● **Reproductions** of antique book ends, furniture; and busts of
ancestors made to order. These come with a Certificate of
Authentication from the Museum of your choice; much in demand
from Reproduction Tudor mansions.

● **Cordon Bleu Cuisine**. Personal catering services deliver Grouse *en
croute*, *Escargot fumé au truffe*, etc. to the *soirées* of the class
conscious. Train your staff at the Masters' School of Servile
Grovelling. Remember to leave the tins in the liveried Ford Transit
outside.

● **Soft furnishings**. Exclusive designs hand-stitched by craftsmen to
the client's own specifications. You can use the same goods as the
'Amazing clearance bargains at slashed prices!' for *Exchange and*

Mart, but substitute tasteful regency stripe for glossy pink plushene.

● **Old Apothecary Brand Shampoos.** This is one of my own lines that does well at Christmas. A heavy glass bottle carries a picture of an old wiseacre gleaning miraculous herbs from the sward. I make the preparation from Glosso® detergent, into which I toss a handful of mint. *Le Vicompte de Charisme* male preparations are similar, but substitute cloves.

● **Rent-a-butler.** You supply old-fashioned retainers to receive guests at the estates of the Nouveau Riche. They come complete with a set of names of old-established aristocracy to drop in front of guests that the clients wish to impress. They are called 'Perkins' or 'Mathers'. Your butlers can be recruited from the ranks of the old-established aristocracy whose stately homes are now occupied by the Nouveau Riche.

THE MASTERS' RULES FOR ADVERTISING

● If it is cheap it is an unrepeatable offer; if it is expensive it is a limited edition.

● People will pay more for a bargain.

● The bigger the price, the smaller the typeface.

● Class is paying more for what other people cannot afford to pay less for.

HOW TO MAKE
MILLIONS
FROM BEAUTY AND HEALTH

Most people are worried about their appearance, and with good reason. It is only on rare occasions that Nature bestows the kind of classic symmetry of features with which I am blessed. Human vanity is a rich field for those who wish to plough a profitable furrow. Most women seem to think they are too fat, and some of them even have a weight problem as well. Men generally want to learn how to kick sand into the faces of other men, and have a cleft chin like Kirk Douglas. There has been a recent tendency for growth in the Do-it-Yourself approach to Health and Beauty, which can only be deplored by experts like myself who know that getting really fit and attractive is an expensive matter. It is hardly possible to go down to the off-licence without being knocked down by hordes of joggers. Fortunately, many of these are getting run over by articulated lorries or suffering heart attacks. Nobody who has stayed on my Health Hydro on the Lanarkshire Fells has yet been run over by an articulated lorry, although I admit a few have had heart attacks trying to scale the walls.

To produce the perfect physical specimen in mind and body is one of the noblest means by which to become Extremely Rich. Your pile of cash has been rendered from a mountain of flab and fat. The pounds in your pocket are a metaphor, to borrow a term from Poetry, for the pounds that your clients have shed at your behest. Fortunately, it is very easy to make a million from being an expert in Beauty and Health by following the Rules I have developed over the years. There is no need to go to the lengths of my friend Jarvis, whose Senna Pod diet led to the famous Banstead Belsen case, which was given somewhat unfavourable coverage in the Press. The Golden Rule is: 'What's good for the body is good for the Pocket.' When you have made enough money you can maintain your own Beauty and Health by a diet of smoked salmon, fresh strawberries and champagne, which is low in calories and high in nutrition.

HEALTH FARMS

Any remote croft in the south-east of England is an ideal site for establishing a health farm. The idea is very simple: people pay you a great deal of money to stop the things they most enjoy doing, so that when they leave they can enjoy doing them again with a clear conscience. Peace of mind is assured by doing the decor in pastel green and by having potted plants around, which makes people feel close to Nature. They get lots of exercise from bicycles that stay in the same place. Every six hours they are given a carrot to chew on. On Sunday they are given a whole plate of carrots. This means that the catering side of a health farm is pretty cheap to run, particularly if you grow your own carrots.

Sauna treatment is an essential part of the course. This consists of a number of separate stages:

- Clients are strapped into small boxes which are heated to enormous temperatures by burning pine chips. This is to open up the pores. When your clients turn a rich purple colour, like an over-ripe strawberry, usually after an hour or so, they are ready for,

- Complete immersion in ice-cold water, or, if the weather is especially bad, a naked roll in the snow. This is to close up the pores. When the clients turn a rich blue colour, resembling an over-ripe plum, they are ready for,

- Being beaten with bundles of birch twigs.* This is to close up the

* Real Scandinavian birch twigs are sometimes difficult to get near Bexhill. Fine imported twigs are available from:
   Morsters Health Imports,
     Greedenveien 13b,
       Cønjob,
         NORWAY.

pores for ever. Do not worry if guests finish up a patchwork of black and blue colours after this stage of the treatment; they know it is doing them good.

In my experience most clients hardly have the energy to crawl off to collect their carrots after a few hours in the sauna.

Most of your guests will need to be pummelled and beaten on their spare tyres every day. Retired boxers make especially suitable staff for this treatment.

Any clients who still have pores left after a week should be rolled in mud. This also removes any impurities in the skin.

Money-Making Hint. Your clients will be desperate for food or booze after a few days of the above. Your Contraband Steward supplies them with Mars Bars for £5 a go, or with miniatures of El Cid Spanish brandy for a tenner. A few days later you discover the deception and publicly fire your Contraband Steward. This is all part of the cure, because your clients feel so guilty they gladly surrender their carrot ration and redouble their efforts on the trampoline. Film shows are played every night. These consist of pictures of scrumptious cream cakes and bottles of Courvoisier VSOP. Anybody found salivating fails to get their evening carrot.

After two weeks the surviving clients are given a slice of toast, and some herb tea to purify what remains of their blood.

Important note Some long-term guests get so weak they can scarcely sign their cheques. Always have some good, nourishing beef tea available in case this happens.

> 'MONEY MAY NOT BUY YOU HAPPINESS BUT IT GIVES YOU A BIGGER RETURN ON YOUR UNHAPPINESS' R.M.

DIETS

An even simpler way to purvey the Body Beautiful is to let your customers in on the secret of a diet which will help them lose their unwanted pounds en route to your pocket. Most of the fat in the world today is due to lack of Roughage. The reason you do not see many obese gazelles is because they eat lots of grass, which is full of roughage. This is why I plan to launch the NEW BRAN BAR under the slogans, 'Learn to Love the Loo' and 'Finest Tunisian dates and

Israeli almonds, nestling in a bed of bran gleaned by rustics from the fields of Kent, all covered in rich, Milk Chocolate, will add emotion to your motions.'

Now that science has turned its attention to the problems of the Overweight it is possible to devise a whole series of diets which are fully approved by the Medical Profession, and guaranteed to work. The most important discovery was that eating fat makes you thin. This has led to the following exclusive diet which you may use as the basis for your crash course in weight loss:

	Breakfast	Lunch	Supper
Day 1	Pig fat	Chicken fat consommé	Pork fat rissoles
Day 2	Dripping au naturel	Goat's lard bonne femme	Chicken fat consommé
Day 3	Boiled pig fat	Chicken fat consommé	Lamb fat chunks fried in dripping
Day 4	Steamed pig fat	Sweet and Sour Fat	Chicken fat consommé
Day 5	Dripping-fried dripping chunks	Chicken fat consommé	Goat-and-pig fat salad with crackling
Day 6	Chicken fat consommé	Fat aux fats	Deep fried crispy fat
Day 7	Fat	More fat	Fat again

This diet has proved 100 per cent effective in inducing weight loss among my thousands of satisfied customers. My only failure was a particularly hard case who was last heard of living in a sty just outside High Wycombe.

Acceptable names for your slimming company:

Sylphs Ltd

The Thin Man Corp.

Skinny Lizzies

Figure It Out Ltd

The Scientific Trim and Slim Organisation

Unacceptable names for your slimming company:

Porkers Anonymous

The Grossly Overweight People's Reduction Society

The Lovable Fatties Group

Face Stuffers

Gobblers

Once you have established your clientèle, you should reward every 3lb of weight lost by the gift of an elegant little figurine in the shape of a leaping impala. On the other hand, those who have put *on* weight, be it so little as ½ oz, will be given a lumpy model of a pig, which makes greedy, slurping noises whenever it is jiggled.

All the staff in your head office should be picked for their exceptional thinness. Out-of-work actors, who often haven't eaten for months, are highly suitable, and moreover usually accept appropriate skeleton wages. You fit the kind of fairground mirrors in the waiting rooms that convert the ordinary figure into a portly barrel. Because most of your customers will already look like portly barrels this will induce the right frame of mind for parting with large sums of money.

The more you charge, the more likely you will be to attract Celebrities. I can confidentially tell you that many of the well-known faces on TV quiz shows have weight problems with their bodies as well as their minds.

Of course, all that fat does tend to be a little short of nutrition. This means that you can sell courses of vitamin supplements* at £3 a tablet, which is a guaranteed way of swelling the coffers. Vitamin C is a particularly profitable item because you can buy the pills for 35p a gross from Boots. Charging such a lot makes your clients aware of what a delicately balanced organism their body really is. They will leave with a new respect for their metabolism, which is the word we experts use for 'what goes in, must come out'.

> 'NEVER CRY OVER SPILT MILK – BUY THE COW' R.M.

Important. Few people are blessed with the kind of perfect proportions and compact, yet lithe figure that Nature vouchsafed to me in the Lottery of Life. If you have a tendency towards bulging thighs or pendulous gut, you should *keep away* from head office at all times. This will not be much of a problem once you are established.

* Finest vitamin courses available from:
  Mastervite,
  5, The Jitterings,
  Newcastle upon Tyne NE4 6HR.

MUSCLES

Most of the people who do not want to lose flab want to gain muscles. These muscles enable them to lift huge weights, wiggle their biceps and kick sand in the face of their rivals. I have acquired amazing muscles myself: I have often noticed that the quivering of my biceps produces extraordinary effects on members of the opposite sex. Sometimes their members even quiver back at me. Body building is now pursued by thousands of men who wish to impress by sheer bulk, and want to do interesting things with their tibias.

Because most of the work of body building is done by the clients themselves, your money-making role is directed towards providing them with the equipment essential to coax their muscle into full bloom. Most of this equipment consists of heavier and heavier weights; by the time you can lift the biggest one your muscles simply *have* to be bigger than they were when you started.

My friend Jarvis (whose muscular development relates to those manual muscles which can be used to count used notes) scored a notable Money-Making Scheme with his 'All-in-one for bigger biceps – only £3.95 p&p.' 'Within three weeks you will be able to run to the top of a six-storey building with a sack full of bricks', he promised. The £3.95 purchased the sack. The written instructions were to put one brick in the sack the first day and run to the top of a six-storey building, two the second day, four the third day, eight the fourth . . . etc. The only snag came when some of the clients who had completed the course decided to return the sack (and the bricks). Jarvis spent some pleasant weeks convalescing on his South American *estancia*, in the company of a young lady contortionist from Bertram Mills circus.

Simple instructions for becoming Enormously Rich from Muscle Equipment:

● Always use a 'Before' and 'After' series of pictures. It is sometimes a problem finding the right 7 stone (132 Kg) weakling for the 'Before' picture, who should not only be remarkably weedy, but should also wear enormously thick spectacles. I have often found the perfect specimens in the Mathematics departments of some of our older universities. The 'After' picture can be any one of your good-sighted star pupils, equipped with a suitable wig.

● Muscles are made of protein, so Scientists tell us. This means there is a huge market for muscle-building Elixir, compounded to a recipe known to such Ancient Greek strong men as Hercules and Adonis. I have found a mixture of dried milk and soy bean flour can be sent through the post without much trouble.

● Ladies have now taken up this healthful pastime so there is a good sale for 'His 'n' Hers Weight sets'. Hers are like His only smaller.

● Always offer those vital accessories: Tarzan leotards ('straight from the upper reaches of the Orinoco'), Safety-First Crotch Bulges ('add endowment to your proportions') and Sand (for kicking in faces). A full wholesale list can be obtained from:
> The Incredible Hulk,
> Back Passage,
> Runcorn Road,
> Colchester CO8 4RZ.

MENTAL HEALTH

A perfect body without a mind to match is a hollow shell. Fortunately for those of us with compassion and a genuine pecuniary motivation there is still much misery in the world. A lot of this is due to Wrong Treatment when people were too small to remember what the Wrong Treatment was, and naturally this leaves them confused. Psychiatrists discovered that unlocking these distant memories made the psychiatrists very well-heeled, producing the means to live in large houses in tree-lined streets in Golders Green, and sometimes cheered the patients up as well. This is why there are now so many psychiatrists. They often have degrees from ancient Seats of Learning in Austria, but as Erroll Flynn once said, you can learn as much from the School of Hard Knocks.

> 'GOLD DOES NOT GROW ON TREES – IT HANGS AROUND IN BARS' R.M.

1 OLD-FASHIONED TREATMENT

Setting up as a Therapist (the Law will not allow you to call yourself Doctor) has lots of advantages for those who wish to relieve distress in their Fellow Men. In the first place you are paid by the hour, which means you can knock off for lunch or a game of billiards whenever you feel like it. Then again my constant experience is that the richest patients are those with the Wrong Treatment which is hardest to unlock, which means many hours of therapy and many £££s. Some of these problems even go back into the womb, which is a very difficult place to reach. The equipment is very simple: an antique couch, and an eighteenth-century globe on a mahogany stand. The couch is for the patients to lie on, and the globe is for you to twiddle slowly while they are talking. The more talking they do and the less you do the better the treatment. If you are very successful you may even need two globes.

A **word of warning** here. People with Troubled Minds come in two main types: the neurotic and the psychotic. These are technical terms we wizards of the cerebral cortex use for what are generally known as nervous wrecks and loonies respectively. ONLY EVER TREAT NEU-ROTICS. You can easily tell the difference with a little practice. Neurotics bite their nails and have bags under their eyes and always ask how much you cost, whereas psychotics have glassy stares, and go on about how they are going to conquer Europe when the Duke of Wellington is assassinated, or how they are being persecuted by Michael Parkinson via the TV waves. They never seem much con-cerned about your hourly rate. Few psychotics have very much money because they are completely round the bend, except for one or two who are dictators of South American republics. Neurotics are often very affluent and guilty about it which makes them very keen on spending their money on you giving them the peace of mind that only comes with spending their money.

Once you have treated one wealthy neurotic your problems are over: you get more patients by word of mouth. If you have a name like Eric Normal or Rich Forthright it is a good idea to adopt a Professional Name like Samuel Greenberg or Sigmund Finkelstein as this inspires confidence. Also you should grow a droopy moustache and wear a bow tie, slightly crooked, at all times.

Treatment of mental conditions is now becoming highly Scientific, and you will need to master a number of technical terms when it comes to your diagnosis. Here are a few of the words you will need when describing what a mess your patient's mind is in before fixing the next appointment and taking off for the club:

Oedipus complex State of mind whereby the patient wants very badly to go to bed with his mother (males only). Some of my patients have mothers who must be 80 years old at least. This shows how ill they are.

Electra complex State of mind of female patient who wants to go to bed with her father. Since their fathers are often dead this must be very frustrating.

Depression Gloom – can be *acute* (v. severe) or *chronic* (won't go away). These patients need cheering up.

Manic depression Periods of wild hilarity alternate with deep gloom. Patients often arrive in the hilarious condition and are swathed in gloom by the time they see the bill for the session.

Paranoia Feeling of being persecuted or followed, never trusting anyone. Always insist on COD payment with these.

Trauma Something Nasty buried in the Vaults of the Mind often relating to Big Jobs. Mention of these often induces dramatic reaction in patient, similar to that of receiving bill.

Deep-seated trauma As last, but worse.

Transference Phenomenon whereby the patient comes to rely utterly on the therapist. Most important to show that your relationship is purely professional at this time – e.g. by doubling the bill.

Repression The process of sending the Trauma down to the Vaults.

Analysis The process of getting into the Vaults to find the Trauma.

Catharsis The process of flushing the Traumas out of the Vaults.

Subconscious The Vaults themselves.

You may find it an advantage to adopt a Middle European accent, if you are good at voices. This is the kind of clipped tone used by Concentration Camp Commandants in movies about the Second World War, e.g. Curt Jurgens.*

Important note. Occasionally one of your patients may wax hysterical or attack you with a handbag – 'freak out' as we Nureyev's of the Psyche technically term it. This usually seems to happen near the end of a Session as patients open the small brown envelope presented to them by your attractively tanned Personal Assistant. The sight of a fellow human in true agony of mind is most distressing, and I would recommend having a rear exit to facilitate your safe and easy removal to the restorative atmosphere of the Golf Club.

2 MODERN MONEY-MAKING METHODS WITH THE MIND

If you wish to relieve the Mental Misery of Mankind in a less one-to-one, interpersonal situation there are plenty of new ways to make an honest Venezuelan *escudo* by getting your agonised individuals together in groups. YOU charge a hefty fee for setting up the group, and another hefty fee for letting them out of the group again. This has the advantage that if your patients get *worse* after the treatment you can always blame it on the fact that the rest of the group were bananas.

* To add authenticity you need various knick knacks from Old Vienna, and a complete set of signed portraits of the Fathers of Modern Psychotherapy: Sigmund Freud, Carl Jung, Alfred Adler and Ernest Jones – to leave dotted about your consulting room. These are available from: Psychoanalytic Accessories Ltd, Masters House, Walton-on-the-Naze, Essex.

Group therapy Patients sit in a circle and pour out all their vitupera-
tion and innermost secrets. Occasionally they break off to stab a
pillow or sit on a potty. Your role is to encourage everybody to spill
the beans, or if they are very inhibited to get them to throw up.

After six weeks of this treatment they have the courage to be rude
to their mother-in-law, or else take off to a sheep farm in the centre
of Australia. Either way, it is an improvement.

The Masters' Method. New and sophisticated group therapy methods
are now available, any one of which is full of potential to put you in
the supertax bracket, and buy you that block of villa-ettes in Benidorm. I have combined many of them in a unique, easy-to-use amal-
gam, to which I am proud to give my name:*

● The group are introduced to one another, strip off, and spend
several days feeling over each other's anatomy in a darkened
room, including the dangly bits. After this they won't feel guilty or
prurient about the human body. As a matter of fact, they probably
won't be interested in it at all.

● One by one they are led into the centre of the 'Nest' (for so we
term the Therapy Rooms) where they have to scream at the top of
their lungs until they fall exhausted to the floor. This we call the
ORIGINAL GROAN. This takes us back to our distant tribal days
when we used to do this kind of thing all the time.

● The group is now split up into pairs. Members of each pair take it
in turns to say, 'I'm OK; You're OK; we're both OK' in six-hour
bouts for six days. After this they generally believe they are OK.
Then the lights are suddenly turned on and everyone is smothered
in rose petals. This is a most moving moment, and is what the
Eastern Sages have often referred to as Enlightenment.

● The group is then released into the Garden of Eden, a luxury
hothouse full of pendulous fragrant blooms, trickling fountains and
background Music by Mantovani and the Ronettes. This is an
expensive place to run, so the charge is fairly tasty for this service.
Nobody feels much like leaving as they have not had their clothes
back yet.

● Finally the CEREMONIAL REBIRTH. All clients are stuffed into
plastic wombs in the foetal position. They hatch, transformed, the
perfect butterfly from the crawling grub, to a personal fanfare from
the Huddersfield Lido Brass Band. A presentation of a medallion,

* Franchises available from:
  Masters Psychological Co.,
  Calle Shirle Basse,
  Benidorm,
  Spain.

several Bills, and the Masters' Method is over. A measure of its success is that nobody has ever had to return.

Helpful hint. You have to be on informal first-name terms with your group. You should in fact be known as 'Dave', which is the best all-purpose name. If you happen to have a name like Sigmund Finkelstein or Samuel Greenberg keep it under wraps.

HOW
TO TURN WAR TO
REMARKABLE
PECUNIARY ADVANTAGE

War is one of the easier ways to make a killing. There have been wars for a long time. Most of the old civilisations were either sacked or pillaged, which is why there are no old civilisations around today. This is a good thing, because it regularly kills off the more aggressive persons, so that the businessmen can get on with making lots of money in the peace that follows. Taking part in real combat is a mistake for any entrepreneur. However, there is a lot of money to be made from the sidelines, supplying the bombs, guns, poisonous gases, etc. that go into any war worth the name. War also has the advantage that a lot of the equipment gets bashed around pretty regularly, so that a new supply is always needed. Bombs can be used only once. Wars also tend to *escalate*, which means that if side A throws one bomb at side B, side B immediately wants to throw two bombs at side A, which is good for business.

Beginners tend to feel that the supplying of lethal materials does not conform to the higher echelons of the business ethic. This view is most misguided. Wars these days are mostly fought between factions, one supported by the CIA and the other by the KGB. Both sides are extremists. Extremists are bad for any country, because when they gain power they always chuck out the businessmen essential to any decent society. By encouraging such factions to exterminate one another the dealer in napalm makes a central contribution to purging the country of its most undesirable elements, thereby restoring the freedom of the Ordinary Man to go out and eat in the best restaurants without the fear of being hit by missiles. As an example, take the recent events in Transwana. My friend Jarvis took a keen personal interest in this conflict, a concern not unconnected with the uranium mines. There were two main factions – the left-wing M'Badis and the right-wing M'Gudis. By supplying arms to *both* sides Jarvis ensured that both M'Badis and M'Gudis were reduced to a small minority of the population. Recent reports indicate that some half dozen of either side are still hurling bazookas at one another over a sand dune in the desert. But the main reins of power are now firmly in the hands of the M'Odrets, and the rejoicing population is back at work in the uranium mines, with their 'Jarvisco' corrugated houses and twice weekly leukaemia screenings. Jarvis was presented with the Order of the Charging Rhinoceros, and increased his holding to 73 per cent.

International arms dealers also have an easy passage into countries normally noted for keeping passengers waiting for hours at air terminals. As soon as you appear, excited officials will whip you off to the best hotel, and ply you with one of the three bottles of Chateau Latour in the kingdom. This is a perfect illustration of the principle that *he that supplies a demand can demand a supply.*

> 'NEVER WORK FOR MONEY – LET MONEY WORK FOR YOU' R.M.

To *buy your arms* you need to find a source of supply. Dictators are often the best people to approach, especially those who have had absolute power for a number of years, and survived several assassination attempts. These have often grown tired of killing off their enemies, and even awarding themselves medals begins to pall. Fortunately, at this stage they start to develop *whims*, which means they are consumed by a sudden desire to own Napoleon's bed, Hitler's paintbox, or Marie Antoinette. Your job is to trade these ultimate luxuries for a decent batch of Russian Dsembowlovich rifles or French *Zut* grenades.

A *word of warning* here: NEVER deal directly with the dictator in his own palace. Some of these dictators have been known to develop a sudden whim for beheading European entrepreneurs. My friend

Jarvis had a narrow escape from decapitation after what came to be referred to as the Bombs for Peanuts Scandal. Always meet the trusted agent of the dictator in the Palm Room of the Zeebrugge Heights Hotel, where you can talk business in a relaxing atmosphere over a couple of Bacardis, lulled by soothing arrangements of Swiss clog dances for string orchestras.

To *sell your arms* meet the agent of the appropriate faction the following day. Some of these persons can be a little conspicuous if they come disguised as bushes, or dangling with rhinoceros bones, although others merely wear ill-fitting suits. I usually organise a *rendezvous* in a nearby park, where I identify myself with some pre-arranged verbal signal such as, 'I hear the hibiscus is fragrant in Poona.' *Only trade the arms for money.*

Important. You must never refer directly to the goods in question as guns, grenades, mines, etc. This is indiscreet. I always refer to my commodities as 'pomegranates', which is a kind of fruit.

If you are very fortunate the faction may be in the same country as the dictator from whom you are buying the pomegranates (guns, mines, etc.). Then you only have to shift them a few miles down the road before they are 'captured' by your clients. This avoids a lot of the trouble that you may encounter in *moving your arms*. This is not as difficult as you might believe, however. Most of the countries with the kind of wars of interest to the money-maker have regimes where customs employees have a profound respect for a packet of US dollars left in the *Poste Restante*. They will usually turn a blind eye to large wooden crates marked 'pomegranates – with care'.

If your faction wins the war you are likely to be made a hero of the new Republic of Grabonia; if your faction loses the war the victors are likely to attribute their success to the faulty weapons of the enemy, and you are certain to be awarded the Distinguished Star of Generalissimo Pommadoro. Either way, you should win some big contracts when peace is restored.

Arms come in three main sizes:

Small Can be carried around by one man, and used to bump off one or two opponents; also used for maiming and crippling. These are the best buy for most purposes as they can be moved around in boxes marked 'Tea'.

Medium Guns and the like which are trundled around by several men, and can be employed to dismember a dozen or more opponents. These can be a bit expensive, because nowadays they are equipped with sophisticated electronic wizardry to help detect

opponents. They can be hard to conceal, except in boxes marked
'lions for export'.

Large Battleships, tanks, A-bombs, etc. needing special crews to
man them, and generally designed to blow places off the map and
clobber other equally expensive items. These are not a practical
proposition for the average entrepreneur. Not only are they
inordinately expensive, which puts them beyond the reach of the
factions who are the usual customers, but they also tend to cause
International Incidents and spark off major conflicts, in which you
might get hurt.

In general I would confine your attention to the small items. They
are the ones used in *guerilla* warfare, which is the kind in which
soldiers dressed in bandannas leap out from behind bushes and hurl
Coke bottles full of model airplane glue. Most small insurgent groups
can fork out for a few dozen Russian Goreskaya rifles; they occasionally capture one of the large weapons by driving the Russian oper-
ators mad with their incessant chanting of patriotic fighting songs.
It can be rather difficult to make contact with guerilla leaders because
they creep about the place disguised as herbs. If you master the
words of the patriotic fighting song, which invariably translates as:
'Death to the Oppressors and Victory to the People's Liberation
Army', you can often identify one of the guerillas when a nearby tree
joins in the chorus. If it shoots you, however, it is probably a tree
belonging to the right wing.

MAKING AN ARMS DEAL

I avoid going into the field of combat, because of the danger of being
mistaken for someone who does not have the interests of the People
at heart. Fortunately, it is possible to do a lot of lucrative arms dealing
without stirring from the first-class hotels with private solaria that
are your customary place of repose. As with most deals requiring
delicacy of touch and absolute secrecy, it is necessary to be *discreet*
and to blend with the crowd. Because most of the people staying at
top-rate hotels in Zurich are other arms dealers this is not difficult.
You should be known only as Mr Percival. You should be on the
alert for government spies, who look much like the other arms
dealers, but are recognisable because they always covertly examine
their drinks bill.

MEN AT ARMS

Most fighting is done by soldiers. Nowadays some of the left-wing soldiers are women; on the right wing, the women are generally left at home to slave over a hot stove. A lot of the soldiers belonging to factions are volunteers, but a few join up because they like wading through swamps. Nearly all of these military persons are amateurs. Amateurs can do pretty well at maiming and killing if they are in the right mood, but there is still no substitute for the skill and dedication of the professional. These are not men who start spraying a sten gun around in all directions at the first sniff of an enemy. They have been disciplined for many years by officers who have had expensive private educations. They have learned to recognise that brains are an encumbrance to a military superior. Most factions realise that it is a great help to have a few of these professionals fighting by their side. They are even willing to pay large sums of money in an appropriate currency to get the comrades they want. YOU can be the agent to supply this valuable human resource.

Fortunately it is not a difficult matter to find dedicated, professional soldiers who will throw in their lot with the local Liberation Army on the promise of a couple of gold bars. Many of these have left the Regular Army, some rather suddenly. They may be officers who have been caught with their hand in the till (*cashiered*) or they may be sappers bored with years of buffing their boots in the depths of East Anglia. They may yearn for a bit of real action in the far reaches of the African bush, or they may feel that their disembowelling technique is getting a bit rusty from months of loafing around in peace. It is not difficult to find out who has left the Army, and the important thing is to make your Tempting Offer to them before they start getting bit parts in TV series about disembowelling or silent strangulation.

> 'MONEY CAN'T BUY YOU LOVE; BUT IF YOU SPEND ENOUGH ITS
> HARD TO TELL THE DIFFERENCE' R.M.

Once you have secured your fighting force they are sent first class to the nearest country sympathetic to the factions they are to fight for. Here they join their comrades and march off into the tsetse-infected night for as long as the money lasts. They should be WARNED never to address their comrades as 'nig-nogs' or 'dagos', as their employers may find this offensive, especially if they are fuzzy-wuzzies or wops. You should keep your own contact with your recruits to a minimum, because they may blame YOU for their misadventures. There is nothing worse than being dismembered by a mercenary crazed by yellow fever or hookworm. Remember, Discretion is more lucrative than Valour, and an alias costs nothing.

Finally: never trust a mercenary who is not interested in the money. He is probably a fanatic, and fanatics can be dangerous.

GETTING A PIECE OF THE ACTION

Even in war, life must go on. For those with a sensible degree of cupidity there are plenty of opportunities to grow rich, even as the shells whizz overhead. War only serves to intensify demand for all the little luxuries that titillate the palate and fit on top of *canapés*. During the recent troubles in San Mogadon the imports of caviare and vintage champagne hit a new high. The allure of these tasty extras is only increased by the knowledge that the population as a whole is strictly rationed to a diet of soybeans and carrots. YOU can be responsible for keeping civilised tastes alive under these distressing circumstances. Any man who could have got a supply of soused herrings into the Berlin Bunker would have made his fortune, because the Führer would have been only too happy to trade in a lot of his loose gold for a nibble on his favourite savoury as the Third Reich got into serious trouble. Crisis stimulates the taste buds as much as it loosens the purse strings.

The only problem is getting the articles to where they are needed. This is not very different from moving arms, except that people are more likely to eat the contents. Sometimes the normal smuggling routines run into a bit of trouble; for example, when I attempted to import Gorgonzola to satisfy the beleaguered cravings of the Shiraz of Grabonia one of the customs officials was asphyxiated in the bonded warehouse while on night shift. I have found that marking boxes with 'Urgent – Save The Children Fund' often does the trick (although the occasional box is broken into by people with an insatiable craving for jelly babies).

WAR IN A WORD

- It takes two to make a quarrel; it takes three to make a profit.
- When Left fights Right there is a deal in the Middle.

- Small arms are Big Business.
- There is Money in being Mercenary.
- Death sharpens the palate; champagne is the natural foil for the Molotov Cocktail.

HOW TO BECOME
EVEN RICHER
WHEN EVERYONE ELSE GOES
TO THE WALL

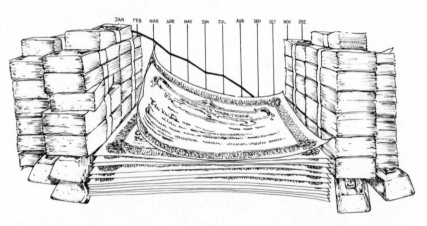

You do not have to be an Einstein or a Mortimer Wheeler to see that the World Economy is in trouble. Inflation is inflating and depression is depressing. Even successful entrepreneurs and grey eminences like myself are having to desert the Gaming Tables of Monte Carlo and show up at the office once or twice a month. Others have been known to jump from high windows of office blocks belonging to international corporations, frequently with unpleasant results. This is known as Loss of Confidence. It produces high unemployment, especially among the most important sector of the work force employed as waiters in French restaurants like Le Cochon in Marylebone Square.

All this might look like bad news for devotees of the High Denomination Bill, but this chapter proves that the opposite is the case. In the words of an old Japanese proverb, 'There is nothing like an earthquake to open up bank vaults.' By following the simple Masters' Plan for Solvency Survival YOU CAN not only weather the coming Storm without becoming involved with any sinking ships or clutching at straws, but will even benefit from the financial demise of others who have not read this book. Until recently I had reserved the information to which I am privy for my personal coterie at Florin-La-Mer, an exclusive *soleil-nid*, not unadjacent to Cannes, to which I am accustomed to retire with employees of the Inland Revenue Service with whom I wish to ingratiate myself. Now, however, I have resolved to lay all before the reader, partly because many of the facts have now been made public by Eugene T. Grasper in his epoch-making volume, *The Currency Crisis: Its Cause and Cure*. The facts are these:

- Within a very few years OR EVEN MONTHS money will enter a period of *Hyper-inflation*. People will be blowing their noses on MILLION POUND NOTES. It will take a fork-lift truck to carry enough ZILLION POUND NOTES to buy a cheese sandwich. Things will be very expensive.

- Everybody will be unemployed, except the Minister for Employment. Queues leading to employment offices will be miles long.

- Local councils and whole towns will go broke, resulting in absolutely no garbage collections and outbreaks of anarchy and violence in schools. Few people will notice much change in this regard.

- Firms will go bankrupt in all directions (except the R. Masters Euthanasia Company Ltd).

- Nobody will be allowed to take any money out of the country. It will be difficult to take anything much anyway without a fleet of fork-lift trucks.

- Shortages will create rationing.

- There will be riots on the streets resulting in a POLICE STATE. Traffic wardens will be allowed to shoot people on sight.

WHY IS THIS ABOUT TO HAPPEN?

All of the trouble is because of the ideas of the infamous economist MILTON KEYNES, who decided that governments ought to interfere with the economy to try to keep everybody prosperous. That this idea is entirely misguided is shown by the fact that ever since the death of Keynes in 1946 the value of money has been falling through the floor and the price of everything has risen through the ceiling. The figure on page 84 shows this beyond doubt.

This slavish following of Keynesian economics has meant that government after government has continued to print more money. That is why these days it is very hard to find any old-looking notes; most of them were only printed last week.

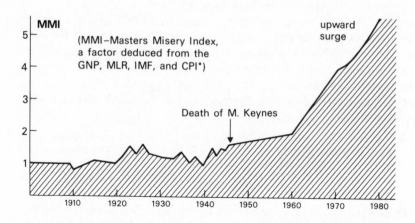

* GNP – Gross National Product; MLR – Minimum Lending Rate; IMF – International Monetary Fund; CPI – Consumer Price Index. These and other terms are explained clearly in a **FREE BOOKLET** obtainable from:

MASTECON Ltd,
P.O. Box 42,
Birmingham 23
(send £5.23 p.&p.).

Not only has the government been printing more money to give higher wages which will buy less because prices are rising at the same time, but they also try to take it back in Taxes. No wonder economies are in a state of confusion. No wonder self-styled pundits get confused trying to explain it all. Those with a true grasp of the complexities of the monetary system are rare birds indeed, and I am one such. The truth is that money has been getting smaller and smaller for some time – it is no surprise that it is buying less and less. Like many simple explanations this seems to have escaped the attention of so-called experts like Jean-Louis Galbraith and Jean-Maynard Freidmann. Only a few years ago five-pound notes were big enough to wrap up a decent lump of rump steak; now you would have difficulty wrapping up a dead sparrow in one of the new ones. The new pound note is even smaller than the old 50p (= 10 bob) note, so it comes as no surprise to *this* Svengali of the Pocket Calculator that it buys so little.

Reliable forecasters (address at bottom of graph) confirm that by 1987 the £ will be worth a mere 8p. Pound notes will be so small by then that they will be sold in books, like postage stamps. They will have glue on the back so that twenty or so may be stuck directly on to a first-class letter.

And do not be fooled that yet more government interference can

84

prevent the cataclysm when it comes. It is no use burying your head in the sand when the tidal wave approaches: only those who have built their portfolio on foundations of solid rock can survive the undermining of rampant devaluation by the grubs and maggots of Lost Confidence.

WHAT ELSE WILL HAPPEN IN THIS TIME OF HORROR AND DESPAIR?

The coming crash will be no respecter of persons: the axe will fall alike on the ordinary tycoon and stars of long-running series on TV. Nobody will believe in money anymore, so that the wads of folding notes that were wont to bring tears of emotion to the eyes of normal persons will become meaningless tokens of a glorious past.

- Even BANKS will FAIL. Cashiers will *beg* customers to accept piles of free money. Don't be fooled: the money is worthless.

- PROPERTY will become WITHOUT VALUE. Nobody will want to buy a house which will become worthless within hours. Titled persons will rush out of Stately Homes to persuade passers-by to purchase.

- Shares and bonds will plunge to new lows. They will even be pulping share certificates to print the *Sunday People*.

- There will be queues MILES LONG to escape to territories OVERSEAS where things are less desperate. One quarter of an acre of good potato-growing land in Peebles will be worth more than the Crown Jewels.

All this may sound pretty discouraging for those with a genuine fascination with living in luxury in pleasant *environs* and mingling with the people who know Andy Warhol. However, the very factors that are going to cause widespread disaster and misery among 99 per cent of the population are also the driving force behind the MASTERS PLAN FOR SOLVENCY SURVIVAL. You will be able to watch the affecting spectacle of millions grovelling in the gutter for discarded crusts secure in the knowledge that it will be your wealth which will be the basis for the eventual re-establishment of the economy. You need the rich to make people rich, just as you need carriers to pass on yellow fever. And like the Black Death, the great Currency Crisis will pass in the manner of all the purifying catharses of history, to rid the world forever of the noxious notions of Milton Keynes so that we may return to the objectivity of the economics of Attila the Hun. Despite all the expert prognoses I am bullish about the future!

THE MASTERS PLAN FOR SOLVENCY SURVIVAL

It is surprising how the simplest ideas are often the hardest to see. No doubt this applied to the discovery of the wheel and the Final Solution. The technique for surviving the Great Troubles to Come is really simple, yet not one person in a thousand has the percipience to see it, even though they are standing on the Edge of the Abyss. You do not have to be a Rasputin of the Ready Reckoner to appreciate the impeccable logic of the Masters Plan. The only question is when to put it into action – my own Guidance Service is available twenty-four hours a day to help those awaiting the Crash. Simply phone: 0978–697823 or write to:

Masters Survival,
  The Bunker,
    Outer Outer Hebrides,
      Scotland.

> 'IT IS BETTER TO GIVE UP YOUR ASSETS THAN TO GET IN THE RECIEVER' R.M.

All you need to survive the coming apocalypse is follow this step-by-step procedure:

- Sell up everything you own. We might make an exception for your Louis Quinze candelabra, but do not keep anything you cannot fit into a small valise. If you have a grandmother now is the time to cash her in. Buy a strongbox. Move into the Salvation Army Hostel for the Penniless.

- Divide all your cash into four piles, which for the sake of argument we will call A, B, C, D.

- With A buy gold coins (G) and put them into your strongbox, which we will call S. Sit on top of it.

- With B buy more gold and put it into a Swiss Bank Account, which we will call Z.

- With C buy some LAND in one of the exclusive areas which will be safe from the ravages of the starving millions (see following section). We will call this land L.

- With D, buy some of the MASTERS DISASTER-PROOF INVESTMENTS listed later in this chapter. Our code for these investments will be M.

The plan is this: When disaster strikes it will be immediately recognisable by a marked lack of people willing to buy you your customary champagne cocktail at the Folie-de-Vie. There will be no Quail *en*

croute at Fortnum's; in fact, there may be no Fortnum's. Max By-
graves will no longer be smiling. As soon as these symptoms display
themselves it is time to move the A in your S to L. This may seem
a difficult thing to achieve because money will by now be so worthless that it will be cheaper to eat it than buy food. This will not worry
you, however, because GOLD will be the new *lingua franca*, and with
it you will be able to buy your way to L. If the government intervenes
by confiscating all gold from private persons, which has been known
to happen when politicians find their own private fall-out shelters
running short of Veuve-Cliquot, this still will not matter because you
have your B in your Z. When you arrive at L bury all the remaining
G from both A and the part you have removed from Z under the
ground in your S, where it will be safe from getting confused with
the S of your neighbour, whose G may be less than yours. Your A
(minus expenses) plus B (except what you have left in Z) will be left
for the future (F). In the meantime you may live on the income from
D invested in M. Nothing can go wrong with this plan.

A **word of warning** here. There may be those who wish to acquire
your G, particularly if you have not been wise enough to establish
your L in one of the Masters Recommended Sites. To this end it may
well be worth your while to purchase a Protective Device such as the
Shrapnel Special which is on offer from Rodco Security, I Fascisti,
Via Malaria, Salerno, Sicily.

You may be wondering why a plan so simple is guaranteed to
WORK, and has been adopted even now by several particularly
prominent dealers in leather goods from Walsall, and by the directors
of more than one fringe bank with which my name has been associ-
ated in the past. For those who have not read my article *Grab while
the going is Good* printed in the *Free Capitalist* here are some of the
questions which most people who wish to retain their regular supply
of smoked salmon *canapés* after the Day of Reckoning tend to ask.

Q: WHAT'S SO SPECIAL ABOUT GOLD?

A. Only gold is as good as gold. Only gold is REAL money. All that
brightly coloured paper stuff is a *chimera*, a figment of the imagination of lackeys enslaved by the distorted vision of Milton Keynes.
Gold can be drawn into infinitely long threads. Gold is incorruptible,
and cannot be attacked by the elements, and an awfully valuable
stash of the stuff can fit into a small leather pouch. In the early 1900s
the average farm labourer was paid one gold sovereign a week: this
is now worth about £70. Ninety-year-old farm labourers who hung
on to their cash are making a killing right now. An old pound note

is only worth about 20p at the moment – so which money would
YOU rather have?

- For centuries alchemists sought to discover the arcane
  Philosopher's Stone which would turn lead into Gold. A few
  probably discovered it, but they did not let on, which is not
  surprising.

- Men have fought wars through History over gold. Nobody has
  ever fought a war over zinc.

- Gold has been fashioned by the great craftsmen of all ages into
  objects of EXQUISITE BEAUTY. These can easily be melted down
  into gold bars when things get tough.

- I am reliably informed that ALL the Gold which has been mined
  through the entire history of Mankind would fit into one large
  room, but it is unlikely that this will ever be proved by actual
  experiment. In any case there is not very much of it about, which
  means it is good news if you have some large lumps of it.

- Gold is the most LIQUID of all assets. This means that it can be
  exchanged without trouble for bottles of vintage champagne in
  any country in the world.

- Gold is the only kind of money which can be used to fill teeth.

- The price of Gold keeps on rising; so does the price of an
  apartment in a fashionable suburb, but the price of gold is not
  affected if a family of alien ethnic origin moves in next door.

So Gold really *is* special. And for those, like myself, with a strong
aesthetic sense and a love of beauty the rich colour of Man's Oldest
Metallic Friend is a source of continuous, inflation-proof uplift; why
else would persons of taste insist on gold accoutrements on the
cocktail cabinet? Remember, when the dollar dithers and sterling
stumbles, only gold keeps your hard-earned cash buoyant *and*
beautiful.

> 'MATERIALISM IS THE GOODS' R.M.

Q: WHY SWITZERLAND?

A: Switzerland is a country of magnificent snow-clad peaks which
have inspired poets to many a line of an inspirational nature. On
lower slopes quaint kine with bells upon their necks wander the airy
glebe, and produce very tasty cheese with holes in like Gruyère and
Emmenthal. But there is more to Switzerland than Heidi and
après-ski. To those of us with an unswerving loyalty to Money,

Switzerland is truly a shangri-la, a secure haven amid the tempes-
tuous squalls which toss the world's financial seas. Many a fortune
wrested from the ungrateful soil of the African continent or brought
in suitcases from the crumbling Italian *palazzo* has found the security
it deserves at last in the anonymity of a Numbered Swiss Account.
The reason for this lies deep in the Swiss Character, a model for us
all to imitate.

- The Swiss have a deep love of Order and Cleanliness. Their
  policemen are firm, but polite, and comprise one in three of the
  population. Switzerland is the only country in the World where
  you can get a ticket for being too slow off the mark at a traffic
  light, which keeps the economy moving.

- The Swiss have a great regard for Stability, which means that they
  don't waste their valuable resources on joining inflammatory
  organisations like the United Nations. They also wisely refrain
  from taking part in any world wars so that they can look after all
  the cash belonging to both sides while these are killing one
  another. They have plenty of Deep Lakes where they can hide all
  sorts of Expensive Items when there is any trouble about.

- The Swiss know that Time is Money. This is why they are so keen
  on making watches.

- The Swiss speak three languages: French, German and Italian.
  This means that they can be on good terms with Napoleon, Hitler
  and Mussolini simultaneously. A lot of Swiss are learning Chinese
  and Russian nowadays.

- The Swiss have a deep respect for Anonymity. The richer you are
  the more anonymous you are. There are plenty of rich and famous
  people in Switzerland who are so anonymous that *nobody at all*
  knows who they are.

- The Swiss have a profound love for their Banks (their biggest
  industry). People who have worked in Swiss Banks for generations
  are sometimes described as Gnomes, and it *is* true that many
  years of lugging heavy gold bars around from one vault to another
  does tend to produce a rather squat stature.

- The Swiss do not have any Underprivileged Minorities. The
  Underprivileged Majority is the rest of the World, who are not
  Swiss.

You need only 5000 dollars to open your Swiss account. There are
plenty to choose from, and I would recommend one that is even
more than usually punctilious about protecting the identity of its
clients. Write to:

Jarvis Schwarz,
Masters strasse 83,
9825 Zurich, Switzerland.

Do not forget to include your cheque for 5000 dollars. I can guarantee that this bank will protect your anonymity. In fact, when you write to them they will probably pretend never to have heard of you.

Q: WHERE SHOULD WE BUY OUR LAND?

A: When the Crash comes it will not be enough to retreat to a cosy *pied-à-terre* in the Home Counties with a lorry load of '54 Armagnac and a complete set of the *Investor's Brittanica*. There may be those who will resent your Prosperity in the midst of Want, who will seem unable to appreciate that it is your prudence in protecting what you have from the ravages of Government Interference that will form the cornerstone of economic recovery. Such is the short-sightedness of Mankind. No, I am afraid that the Masters Recommended Sites will entail a shift from Hearth and Home to an exotic hideaway with subtropical climate, where you will be surrounded by similar survivors of the *Maelström*, with whom you will be able to chat over the electric fence about the current price of Gold and how to obtain Loch Fyne kippers in such troubled times. With these compatible neighbours the Time of Crisis should be whiled away pleasantly enough; you may even find your stay enlivened by Notable Show Business Personalities in the same block.

Fairly safe: The Bahamas. This cluster of Island Paradises lies only 100 miles off the United States. Because there are more than 700 islands there is every possibility of finding your own little hideaway to retire to with the most grateful of your former company secretaries. There are lots of sandy places suitable for burying your gold. My own private Cay of Exploitos is already equipped with a ranch-style shackette, furnished with a leopard-skin and bamboo resterama and a plentiful supply of monogrammed notepaper on which I intend to write my memoirs during the Coming Depression. **A cautionary note** here. There are some businessmen less scrupulous than myself who have sold Bahaman islands of dismal aspect in lots too small to set up a decent table of Coconut Cocktails, let alone a well-appointed shackette. **DO NOT BE TEMPTED** to buy cheap land on the island of Jarvos.

Very safe: Pacific Islands. The Pacific Ocean is an endless expanse of blue water broken only by the occasional shark fin. In the depths of Micronesia lies the exotic island of Moni-moni, which Rodco Security is developing for fugitives from the Horror to Come. The island is protected by mines to stop Gold Pirates. Among other attractions on offer:

- Tasteful colonial-style bungalows surrounded by exotic fruits such as Yam and Sago, with music from *South Pacific* played by a local Combo.

- Room service from grass-skirted *vahines* whose forebears appeared in the celebrated pictures of Paul Gauguin, who also had associations with Banking.

- A Recreation Centre which shows movies of the Stock Exchange, people having long business luncheons at the Clochard Enchainé and sales graphs on the up-and-up, just to ensure the survival of civilised values during the months of isolation.

- The island will have its own paper money for those suffering from withdrawal symptoms from years of handling high denomination notes.

- The admission fee to Moni-Moni is a mere 70 per cent of your hoarded gold, or £150,000, whichever is the greater.

Ultra safe: Private sanctuaries (Masterlands). Even the remote islands of Micronesia appear on maps, if they are big enough. Who knows, governments may decide to invade to steal back some of the Gold which has been rightfully earned by those cashing in before anyone else realised what was going on. There are apparently some people who believe that Gold should be SHARED; little realising that this would result in still worse unemployment after the Crash, because then nobody will have the wherewithal to employ *croupiers*, or bodyguards.

Fortunately there is one haven that is safe from all prying eyes. After the Crash, all the oil rigs will go defunct, because nobody will have enough money to buy any petrol. Rodco Survival has the options to buy these rigs for scrap – but they will be towed to secret sites outside territorial waters in places like the Sargasso Sea where nobody in their right minds ever goes. People who are out of their right minds who find the rigs will be disposed of. The rigs are the *Republic of the Masterlands* (President R. Masters).

The Masterlands will have its own legal system based on the Seven Commandments, or GOLDEN RULES:

- No coveting of neighbours' Gold allowed; anybody found coveting gets the push.

- No coveting of your neighbour's Confidential Personal Assistant either, this resulting in a big fine to the State Coffers.

- No spreading of rumours about the price of Gold falling or

91

otherwise taking the name of Gold in vain. Or else a big fine to the
State Coffers in mint Krugerrands.

● No making of graven images to print duff fivers, even for old
times' sake: everybody knows there is Gold, and only one Gold.
Could result in excommunication on a raft of Coke tins and
expropriation of all wealth by the State.

● Certainly no killing; except by the State Executioner for Violation
of Golden Rule No. 1, when it will serve them right.

● No adultery permitted. Except, that is, by prior agreement between
consenting adults and the exchange of the appropriate number of
Krugerrands with the offended party (see His Masters Voice,
pamphlet no. 27: 'You Will Pay for Adultery' Royal Mint Pubs).

● No working on Sunday. Also on Monday through Saturday. You
can use the air-conditioned recreation facilities seven days a week,
however, to pass the time.

The Masterlands will be a peaceful republic. Everybody gets to commit adultery with everybody else so that the money finishes up the
same as it started, which is the important thing.

The admission fee buys you citizenship for as long as the crisis
lasts, or longer, if you get to like the Sargasso Sea. Outstanding
stories of the survival of Considerable Wealth against enormous In-
flationary Odds will be rewarded by such decorations as the M.C.
(Much Collateral) and the O.M. (Overtly Masterslike); repeated
heroism will receive the Gold Bar.

THE MASTERS DISASTER-PROOF INVESTMENTS

At the heart of every storm there is a still centre where things do not
get bashed about. For every large oak tree that falls in the forest,
twenty small ones spring up to take its place. So it will be with the
dénouement to come. Yes, for those who do not get swept away
headlong into the storm and who keep their eyes fixed on the guiding
star of Profitability, the very uncertainty of the times can be turned
to Good Account. You CAN PROSPER while the Man in the Street
goes to the wall. A few men of perception, among whom I number
myself, have seen the light at the end of the tunnel, and armed with
our guiding principles, you can find your way through the Wilder-
ness to the Golden Age beyond. Not for nothing am I known as 'The
Doyen of the Dow-Jones Index'.

You must remember that even in the midst of hyper-inflation
people *need* things: to turn this intuition into foolproof moneyspin-

ners you just have to pick the right commodity. Here are some of my hot tips:

Candles. Nobody will be able to afford to pay the electricity bill, so this will mark the *renaissance* for the humble candle. Recommended stocks:
Consolidated Wicks
Flame-buoyant Ltd
Rancid and Dripping (Bootle) Ltd
Amalgamated Fats Ordinary Preference.

Property. Although almost all property will become absolutely worthless during the Big Squeeze, there are a few, selected properties which will become enormously sought-after in the time of hyperinflation:

Residential properties sandwiched between butcher's shops or grocers' on the one side and banks on the other. Lucky owners of these properties will be able to fill their wheelbarrows with money and then whizz into the butcher's shop to buy FOOD before the next devaluations, which by then will be only minutes apart. Can you imagine a Rothschild swapping a desirable Eaton Square apartment for a maisonette in Tooting? It *will* happen, so buy now before prices rocket!

Small gold mines. As the price of gold shoots ever upwards, people will go mad for a sniff of the stuff. Buy land *now* in former gold-mining areas. To sell the land simply dress up in old-fashioned white side whiskers, and site yourself in the nearest bar. While puffing at an ancient briar, mumble on about how your grandfather discovered a nugget the size of a hen's egg somewhere 'back out there'. Within hours you will be fighting off the investors. This may be your only chance to acquire an original Van Dyke or Van Rembrandt.

Wheelbarrows. Much increased demand because of necessity of transporting huge quantities of near-worthless notes from bank to butchers, cars being obsolete. Recommended stocks:
Arundel Trundling Co. ordinary issue
Wheelers and Dealers Ltd

Shoe Companies. As previous, death of transport means that stout boots will enjoy unprecedented favour. It is worth digging 90-year-old craftsmen out of retirement *now* to cope with the flood of demand to come. Stockpile for the Crash; you cannot lose.

FURTHER ADVICE

No single book, no matter how brilliant, like this one, can advise you *in detail* about every aspect of your financial survival through the Collapse that is just around the corner. It is with absolute confidence

that I can recommend a number of Consultants whom I have known
personally for many years, and with whom I have many a labyrin-
thine Business Arrangement in the Cayman Islands and Venezuela,
some of them still *sub judice*.

- For *Brokerage Services*: Darrell F. Twister, President, Filbuster,
  Bluff & Bluster, 5791 Rand Street, Diligence, Ill. 45098. Darrell has
  been regularly bullish in a bearish world, though I have not seen
  him for several years, at least not inside territorial waters.

- For *Bullion Dealing*, I can think of nobody other than my old
  associate Midas King, 'Golden Aura', Fandanglos, Bahamas. Midas
  also publishes a fortnightly journal, *International Greed* which is
  available from: Sensible Books, P.O. Box 2367, Gratias y Adios,
  Acapulco 14, Mexico. Regular price £54 per annum, but £65 to
  readers of this book.

- My most trusted advisor on *Tax Shelters*, Hiram T. Shade, has
  gone to a shelter so secure that he is quite unreachable. But I can
  recommend his book *Places to Hide* published by: Very Sensible
  Books, c/o Mr X, *Poste Restante*, Goa.

- For those with a literary/philosophical turn of mind, like myself,
  there are a few texts which should be packed with the Chanel No.
  5 in any suitcase bound for the Lesser Antilles. In particular:

- *Put yourself first*, Norton M. Doppelganger (Narcissus Press,
  £6.99). Explains the meaning of Freedom and Love. A must.

- *A critique of the Keynesian Socio-Economic Model, with Particular
  Reference to the Role of the Individual*, R. Cane (Doppelganger
  Press, £346). A very big book.

- *There's no place like Self*, U.S. Dream (Mailer & Carbuncle, £3.78).
  Takes over where Norton M. Doppelganger leaves off.

> 'A GOOD DEED ALWAYS GETS CREDIT – FOR UP TO TWICE ITS FACE
> VALUE' R.M.

HOW TO MAKE
YOUR FORTUNE
AS AN ENTREPRENEUR

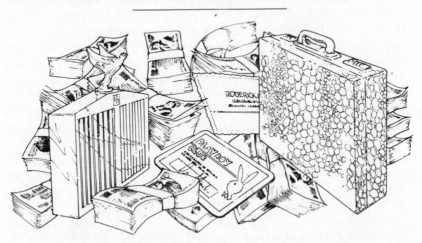

Some people think that the only way to get into the City is to be born into the privileged classes, educated at Eton or Rugby, and to score very poorly in IQ tests. All this is perfectly true. But many years of experience have taught me that the City is not an impregnable citadel. It is there to be stormed by anyone who has taken to heart the Principles that lie behind this book. That this is remarkably easy is one of the Great Secrets of the City. Cleverness is not necessary – after all, the bowler hat was invented to conceal the receding brows of the wearer. All that is needed is to know the rules of the game, to wear a pin-stripe suit, and to be able to remember whether you started a rumour to bring share prices up or send them plummeting down. The entrepreneur is the person who makes things happen; the investor is the person who wishes he could make things happen; while the poor are those who do not even realise that anything is happening. Make sure YOU are the entrepreneur – only the puppet master holds the strings and collects the money when the show is over. Never finish up as a marionette dancing to somebody else's tune, or you may find that your cash surplus has strings attached.

The entrepreneur is the hero of the capitalist world. It is he who skulks in the background of advertisements for Bacardi rum and fur coats. Doormen open doors for him. The sight of his battery of credit cards reduces women to complaisant pulp. He has an impalpable aura that clears tables in exclusive restaurants. For him the law is a plaything to be twisted this way and that much as he used to play with his pet cat as a boy. The press adores him, and invariably describes his most esoteric deals as 'flamboyant'. He alone is permitted to gamble 47 per cent of the Gross National Product in a single night at Gradgrind's. He is redolent with the mystery of Great Wealth, the dark shadow in the dark limousine, cocooned in an atmosphere that rustles with the sounds of expensive silks. The pinnacle of your career as a schemer is to become one of his number. Then you will be able to address cabaret stars and racehorse owners on equal terms, and always command the Presidential Suite at the Hotel Excelsior in Benidorm. Yet the attainment of entrepreneurial status is *not* impossible. The example of my friend Jarvis (now Lord M*****) should be sufficient proof of this. His origins were so humble that even now he blushes to recall the sanitary arrangements of his boyhood. His rise has been far from meteoric (especially in the aftermath of the Thurso Porridge Scandal) and yet now he is spoken of in the same breath as Lord S****** and Lord G******.

> 'NEVER TRUST A MAN WHO CANNOT BE BOUGHT – HE IS ALREADY OWNED BY SOMEONE ELSE' R.M.

Entrepreneurs working in the City make the biggest money with the least effort. This is the reward for previously having made a lot of smaller quantities of money with very little effort. The true entrepreneur does not despise the Small Deal, because he knows it is a stepping stone to the BIG Deal across the River of Liquidity. If he can keep clear of the Bog of Bankruptcy, then the mountains lie beyond! The ways of doing this are as various as the denominations of notes in the Argentine. A few men of true insight, among whom I may count myself, have managed to understand the grand sweep of entrepreneurial ploys. What follows is a digest of the myriad ways to manipulate wealth, a precis in the same class as Perkins's *The Brothers Karamazov in Two Hours* or Figgis's *Bible before Bedtime*.

THREE'S COMPANY, FOUR'S A PROFIT

The unit of financial *legerdemain* is the Company. The Company is an organisation dedicated to profit, and YOU are the managing director. The success of a Company is measured by how rich you become, and how quickly. You are like the Mother Hen, and your Companies are like eggs. Although the eggs cannot hatch without your help, you are certainly not responsible if one of them should go a trifle bad, nor if one of the chicks should scuttle off and get eaten by a cat. You get bigger the more eggs you lay; it often helps you to feather your nest if the eggs never get to hatch at all. Companies die – but the entrepreneur goes on from strength to strength to strength. When you have dozens of Companies the death of one is hardly noticeable – as long as you removed all your interests before the demise.

All you need to start a company is £75 and an idea. Once you have a few other companies you can dispense with the idea. You can buy a company that has ceased trading, like Great Universal Gum Ltd, and change its name to that of your choice – say Masters Holdings (Walsall) Ltd. This is all very simple. There are two ways to start coining large amounts of cash once you have your company: either you start developing your idea, or you start persuading others to invest in your company to make them money. The second is the easier method of acquiring huge sums, because with the first you need to have an idea that works, but with the second you only need people to *believe* that you have an idea which will work. To make the prospects of a company sound convincing enough you need the help of two other people: an expert in the field in which your company operates, and a person of impeccable pedigree, preferably a Lord or a well-known political figure, to appear in bold type on the high quality glossy prospectus. You can usually find an appropriate expert skulking in some university or other. He is delighted to get some free money after all the years of grinding away in poverty to become an expert. The Lord is usually no problem either – I have used Lord Feargus of Casheen many times, but many of the poorer Irish peers are only too glad to get a couple of hundred with no questions asked.

> 'A FRIEND IN NEED IS A FRIEND IN DEBT AT 1% OVER THE BANK RATE' R.M.

Speed is important. You have to discover what the world is short of, then bring your company into existence to fill the shortage. For example, if there is revolution in Colombia, and Colombia is the world leader in Molybdenum supplies, then you will christen your company Molybdenum Research and Development, recruit a famous molybdologist as your expert, and get your City Whisperer to spread rumours of hitherto unknown sources of Molybdenum by the Ubangi. Money will come flooding in. Your shares will rise in price to truly astronomical levels. You may even decide to dispatch a few geologists up the Ubangi to see if there is any Molybdenum there. They might even find some. But the important thing is that your company, which you founded for £75 and a handout to Lord Feargus and Professor Borax, is now worth £600,000. For all the money sent in you have a 5 per cent 'Administration Fee', which is mentioned on p. 123 of the prospectus, in small print half concealed behind a picture of a giant nugget of Molybdenum. This makes you rich. Then you sell the company to a giant mining concern who think you must be on to something because so many investors think you are on to something. This makes you extremely rich, because you have 51 per cent of the shares. Retire to the Bahamas.

The world is always short of something. If there is an earthquake in Belize, coconut matting suddenly becomes sought after; if there is a strike in Melton Mowbray, pork pies are at a premium. The skilful entrepreneur has one company rising as another bites the dust. The important thing to remember is: *Company money is only so much paper*. The increase in value of your company depends on people believing that it is increasing in value; you have to sell before they stop believing in their belief. This is a matter of timing; and skill and timing sorts out the true entrepreneur from the man with the cheap cigar and the nervous tic. Follow the old Podolian proverb – 'the birch is strongest when the sap is rising' – which has been my guide through many a cliff-hanger. Once you have sold, you have the *real* stuff: the comforting bundles of notes bound for the tax haven, or the glittering prizes of mint krugerrands nestling in their dark and secret hole in the Chilterns. You are trading in hope, which is one of the few Commodities without a Quotation, except that it springs eternal. Keep one step ahead and you will never fall one step behind.

SHARES AND A DELUSION

You can see now why it is better to be on the inside making shares, than on the outside buying them. If you are intent on becoming Rich the stock market is not the easiest place to do it from scratch; you need money to make money. Shares in giant corporations yield a few per cent, which is not the stuff of which fortunes are made, and this book is all about making fortunes. Once you are on the *inside* you join the whispering gallery, where the boys tell you whenever something is going to take off, and you in turn let them in on the secrets of Transylvanian Borax. You also know when to jump off the bandwagon before the bubble bursts. A couple of hundred years ago everybody started buying tulips and the price went rocketing up millions per cent. The man on the inside sold his stock *before* everybody else realised they were just boring old bulbs. Life has got more sophisticated since then, with computers, Industrial Indexes and new stripy tulip hybrids, but the same, fickle principles apply. It is better to travel gainfully than to arrive: there is no Cash in a Crash.

A MAN OF PROPERTY

Property is buildings. These are large structures with windows, which house office workers. Building and demolition run hand in hand, like Jekyll and Hyde. Money is made by demolishing one set of buildings and putting up another set of buildings, only higher. Very high buildings are particularly good because you can get lots more people into them and put a revolving restaurant on top. This is one of the fields of endeavour where the money-maker can feel truly *creative*. The urge to Build is one of the primal instincts of Mankind ever since Rameses II used two million slaves to build the Sphinx.

This was the first example of Speculative Building, and people have been speculating about it ever since. The builder has it in his power to change the face of the city, to turn dreary, tree-lined boulevards full of irritating pigeons into iridescent pinnacles, aglow with a thousand fluorescent strips. You can then move out to a mansion in the country, from which you can see your towers on a clear day.

Property development falls into three phases: acquisition, demolition and construction. These three phases always happen one after another.

● **Acquisition** means buying a run-down terrace which you get cheap because it is full of tenants, and then allowing it to fall down so that you get vacant possession. This requires very little effort.

● **Demolition** may be achieved by the last phases of acquisition. More usually it is necessary to hit the property with heavy weights. The last tenants tend to move out at this stage. Sometimes, if the buildings are old, they are *listed* (put on a list) which means that Sir John Betjeman has written some verses about them. Such buildings always seem to ignite spontaneously, and blaze with the burning passions induced by the poetry.

● **Construction** is the job of your Building and Construction Division. It is preceded by planning permission, which is given by a local authority anxious to recoup the Rates they lost when the old buildings keeled over. Buildings are usually tall, oblong structures plated in glass. They have a simple grandeur and *hauteur* appropriate to the age of 14 per cent Unit Trusts. It is very important that each one should have an Artistic Feature placed in the middle of the concrete forecourt. Sculptures are popular for this purpose. I especially recommend the work of the Swedish sculptor, Knut Blok, who produces tall, oblong structures plated in glass.

Once you have built your edifices, you advertise them as superior office accommodation. It is a good idea to keep them empty because that way you can keep putting up the rents. This will make the office blocks extremely valuable, so that you can sell out to another property company which thinks that the rents can be even higher. Thus you become extremely rich. With your money you buy *two* run-down terraces. This is such an easy way to join the ranks of senior entrepreneurs that it is not surprising that many schemers have got into the act. Fortunately all these property companies require office accommodation, which is supplied by other property companies knocking down run-down terraces. So at last all the old buildings are removed and everybody is rich; this is known as *urban renewal*.

With your money you then improve your own personal *estancia* on the outskirts of Esher. This is good for the personalised swimming pool business, and for the men who hang gaily coloured lights between trees. Nobody loses. A *helpful tip* here. It sometimes happens that the early stages of development are hampered by *Residents Associations*. These may try and stop demolition by throwing their babies in front of bulldozers, etc., which is annoying. Identify the ring leaders. These are usually young persons with staring eyes and nowhere to live. Offer them one of your small *pied-à-terres* in Hampstead. The remaining aged and infirm will be no problem.

FAST BUCKS FROM LAME DUCKS

Companies, like people, can get ill. When this happens a Specialist is called in to examine the Cash Circulation, probe the Vital Organs and lop off the odd superfluous appendix. This is very profitable, and requires no medical training. YOU are the *troubleshooter* and doctors always charge hefty fees. The procedure is very simple:

● You are appointed managing director with *Carte Blanche* at a huge salary.

● You borrow great sums of money against the remaining assets of the Company.

● You employ your Own Management Consulting Company to advise on what needs to be chopped. You chop it, and convert the choppings into cash. Pay your Management Consulting Company from the money raised from 2 and 3.

● **Keep up appearances**. This means giving expensive banquets for prospective clients and your Personal Assistants in the Management Consulting Company. There is nothing like the sight of people spending money to convince other people that there is money there to spend.

● When the Company goes bankrupt you arrange for the purchase of all the remaining assets by your Liquidation Purchasing Company. This means you can buy various plant, etc. very cheap, which is useful when you are persuading the next Company to have you as their troubleshooter.

● **Leave town quickly**.

Remember, a dead duck is better than a lame duck. Only then can new, vigorous companies spring into life. The troubleshooter is both mortician and midwife, so he *deserves* to pick up all the cash that is lying around on both counts. A quick death is kinder than a lingering one, and without death there can be no rebirth, unless it is a Nationalised Industry.

THE RICH SHALL PROSPER

The burden of this chapter is: In your formative phase you seek money, but once you have become an entrepreneur *money will start looking for you*. Unto him that has shall be given, but unto him that has not, even that which he has will tend to break down a couple of days after purchase. Once you have confirmed your reputation as an entrepreneur you will be amazed at the way strangers will offer you brown paper parcels stuffed with high denomination notes, confident in your ability to double the money in a few weeks (even allowing for your usual 73 per cent commission). Once you have your ear to the ground in the City, you will be able to found a *Fringe Bank* with impunity, offering giddy interest rates to investors, armed as you are with your agility for leaping on to bandwagons before they crash into liquidity problems. It is all a question of confidence: *confidence is other people believing you can do it, and you knowing you can get away with it if it goes wrong.* Confidence, like money, is something you cannot have too much of. Confidence has buoyed me through many a lean period when the schemes seemed to be teetering on the edge of disaster. Even the humblest schemes in this book are designed to build up your confidence: as the Japanese proverb puts it 'A *yen* under the *bonsai* is a crock of gold beneath the cedar'.

There is nothing more satisfying than being Extremely Rich, other than being Richer Still. This book has demonstrated how easy this is. Sweat alone does not make money; it only leads to perspiration. Keep cool and confident. Nothing profits a man who cares nothing for profits. Always remember, *the World is your oyster:* it is only a question of picking out the pearls from the dross.

> 'HARD WORK IS NO SUBSTITUTE FOR SOFT SELL' R.M.

FURTHER READING

If you have reached this far, you are probably rich enough by now to have the leisure for a good read. The books listed here are a few of those which have stimulated feverish scheming over the last few years. Take along a tome or two next time you are buffing up your brass plaques in the Caymans: reading can be a wise investment of your time, provided you stick to books about money, getting rich, the lives of the wealthy, and the like.

Greed: A Panegyric, Ayn Kruger-Rand (Spitalfield and Shekelstein, £9.50). Full of real poetry. Also some good methods for doubling your turnover.

Howard Hughes: The Myth Behind The Mask, Norton M. Doppelganger (Fab, Faber & Fabest, £2.45). The inside story – from the man who sterilised *his* ice cubes.

Money, Sex and Power: A theological view, Father Thyme-Lyffe (Higher Values Press, £54.76). A fine serious read, with hints on VAT and getting through eyes of needles.

The Usury of Literacy, Silas Braggart (Valuable Books, £5.68). All the dirt on the earnings from Great Books from Homer to Leon Uris. A must for all those who, like myself, like a little literary gravy with their monetary meat.

From Russia with Trove, F. D. Lanes (Defoliation, £4.00). The fascinating story of getting rich from Russian relics, by the leading Ikon Man.

Apotheosis and Statis: A Neo-Popperian Weltschmerz, Lev Cerebrum (Einstein & Bohr, £5.42). A light-hearted guide to the Futures Market.

The Gremlyn Complete All-Colour Guide to High Denomination Bills, Bill Mattock (Gremlyn, 89p). All the World's classics (like the 15,000,000 cruzieros) in living colour, with bits of text in the holes between pictures.

Money, Power and Sex: a new psychic synthesis, Dr Willi Pfennig (Buzzard & Phalarope, £456). The startling new theory of the mind, which relates all traumas to early monetary deprivation.

Taking Stock, Arnold Shrubsole (Broadmoor Books, £3.45). Autobiographical reflections by the noted City embezzler.

Making a Killing, Sergio 'Weasel Face' Gumboilioni (Cosa Nostra Literati, £5.78). A straight-from-the-shoulder guide to getting rich – *fast*.

The A. J. Ayer Bumper Investment Guide, A. J. Ayer (Oxford University Fast Buck Series, 99p). The logical guide to positive thinking on the Stock Exchange.

> 'THE TRUE ENTREPRENEUR KNOWS HOW TO TURN THE THIN END OF THE WEDGE INTO AN OPENING' R.M.

INDEX

NOTES FOR YOUR
OWN MONEY-MAKING SCHEMES

NOTES FOR YOUR
OWN MONEY-MAKING SCHEMES

> 'MEN AT SOME TIME ARE MASTERS OF THEIR FATE;
> THE FAULT, DEAR BRUTUS, IS NOT IN OUR STARS
> BUT IN OURSELVES . . . .'
>
> William Shakespeare, *Julius Caesar*